REFUTING EVOLUTION

A HANDBOOK FOR STUDENTS, PARENTS, AND
TEACHERS COUNTERING THE
LATEST ARGUMENTS FOR EVOLUTION

100,000 in print

REFUTING EVOLUTION

A RESPONSE TO THE NATIONAL ACADEMY OF SCIENCES' TEACHING ABOUT EVOLUTION AND THE NATURE OF SCIENCE

JONATHAN D. SARFATI, PH.D., F.M.

Master Books

First printing: May 1999
Seventh printing: October 1999

ISBN: 0-89051-258-2
Library of Congress Number: 99-70693

Cover Design: Brandon Vallorani
Layout: Diane King

Printed in the United States of America.

Please visit our website for other great titles:
www.masterbooks.net

ACKNOWLEDGMENTS

I thank the following people for reading drafts of this book and making many helpful suggestions (in alphabetical order): Dr. Don Batten, Russell Grigg, Ken Ham, Christine McMillan and Dr. Carl Wieland.

I also appreciate the special advice of Dr. Danny Faulkner on chapter 7 and Dr. Andrew Snelling on chapter 8.

TABLE OF CONTENTS

FOREWORD

I vividly recall a seminar where a young lady, who appeared quite distressed, came up and blurted out "I'm angry."

"At me?" I replied, wondering what sort of tense situation was going to occur now.

"No, not at you – at my teachers and college professors."

"And why is that?" I asked.

This lady went on to say something like this: "Why didn't they tell me about all this evidence that contradicts evolution? How come they taught me ideas that were discarded, even by evolutionists, years ago? Why didn't they let me consider the evidence put forward by creationists? The way I conduct my life is very dependent on my beliefs about origins. Why haven't I been allowed to hear all this information — isn't that what education is all about?"

I must admit that when I was a teacher in the public school system in Australia, I was frustrated by the fact that many of the text books contained evolutionary teaching that had been discarded years ago by evolutionists themselves. It was also disheartening to find that most teachers seemed to just regurgitate to the students what they had been taught at school and college, and yet many of these ideas were outdated and no longer held by leading scientists.

As I talked with these teachers about this situation, I found most had not had the opportunity to read any of the latest findings. There was no system in place to update teachers on the latest research. Also, probably because of economics, textbooks seemed to take years to catch up with current theories.

As a result of this sad state of affairs, generations of students continue to be indoctrinated in outdated evolutionary theories, not even understanding that such teachings are continually modified and discarded in the real world. Thus, students and teachers alike are indoctrinated to believe evolution is fact, when in reality it is a belief system based on ever-changing concepts.

In recent times in the USA, the prestigious National Academy of Sciences made available to public schools and other institutions a book that supposedly presents the latest information on evolution. This publication is presented very professionally and certainly looks as if it might contain irrefutable evidence for evolution. It is designed to persuade and assist teachers to further indoctrinate their students in favor of evolution, with specific advice on countering anti-evolutionist students.

A creationist scientist, Dr. Jonathan Sarfati, thoroughly investigated the claims of this book. Not only were some of these typically outdated and discarded ideas still presented as fact, but at the very least one could say that some of the information was very misleading. There is also a very subtle attack throughout the book on those who hold to the Christian faith.

A highly qualified scientist, the author also has a formidable and unusually wide-ranging grasp of many other fields of knowledge.

I challenge professors, teachers, and students to not only read this book and consider the claims Dr. Sarfati has made, but to check out the documentation for themselves. If they do this, I believe they too may become "angry" at the way information is being presented to the public in such a lopsided manner.

In my opinion, this new publication is one of the most up-to-date critiques of modern evolutionary theory, one that has been so well researched and documented it will challenge the most ardent evolutionist.

Please consider all the information carefully — after all, what you believe about where you came from affects your whole world view. This is an important topic indeed.

Ken Ham
Founder and Executive Director
Answers in Genesis USA

INTRODUCTION

The National Academy of Sciences (NAS) has recently published an educator's guidebook entitled *Teaching about Evolution and the Nature of Science*. It has been made available to educators throughout America to encourage teachers to incorporate more evolution in their classes and basically teach particles-to-people evolution as a fact. The guidebook states its purpose in the preface:

> Many students receive little or no exposure to the most important concept in modern biology, a concept essential to understanding key aspects of living things — biological evolution.

However, it's hard to believe that "many students receive little or no exposure" to evolution. The whole secular education system in America (and most other countries around the world) is underpinned by evolution. After reviewing a number of biology textbooks in the secular school system, we find they are *all* blatantly pro-evolution. It's also hard to believe that evolution is an "essential concept" in biology, because most "key aspects of living things" were discovered by creationists.

For example, Louis Pasteur discovered that many diseases were caused by germs and showed that life comes only from life, Gregor Mendel discovered genetics, and Carolus Linnaeus developed the modern classification system, to name but a few creationist pioneers of modern biology. Also, many  highly qualified biological scientists of the present day do not accept evolution — their work is not affected in the slightest by whether or not fish really did turn into philosophers.

Refuting Evolution seeks to redress the lopsided pro-evolutionary way in which origins are taught. The NAS guidebook, which is compiled by many leading evolutionists, obviously contains the most up-to-date and major arguments for evolution. Thus, this critique of it addresses current evolutionary theory as taught in colleges, public schools, and as broadcast by the media. *Refuting Evolution* responds to many of the arguments in *Teaching about Evolution and the Nature of Science* so that a general critique of evolution can be made available to challenge educators, students, and parents. At the same time, *Refuting Evolution* gives as much positive information as space permits to defend the creationist position. Thus, it provides a good summary of the arguments against evolution and for creation. It should stimulate much discussion and help students and teachers to think more critically about origins.

CHAPTER 1

EVOLUTION & CREATION, SCIENCE & RELIGION, FACTS & BIAS

M any evolutionary books, including *Teaching about Evolution and the Nature of Science,* contrast religion/creation opinions with evolution/science facts. It is important to realize that this is a misleading contrast. Creationists often appeal to the facts of science to support their view, and evolutionists often appeal to philosophical *assumptions* from *outside* science. While creationists are often criticized for starting with a bias, evolutionists also start with a bias, as many of them admit. The debate between creation and evolution is primarily a dispute between two world views, with mutually incompatible underlying assumptions.

This chapter takes a critical look at the definitions of science, and the roles that biases and assumptions play in the interpretations by scientists.

THE BIAS OF EVOLUTIONARY LEADERS

It is a fallacy to believe that facts speak for themselves — they are always *interpreted* according to a framework. The framework behind the evolutionists' interpretation is *naturalism* — it is assumed that things made themselves, that no divine intervention has happened, and that God has not revealed to us knowledge about the past.

Evolution is a deduction from this assumption, and it is essentially the idea that things made themselves. It includes these unproven ideas: nothing gave rise to something at an alleged "big bang," non-living matter gave rise to life, single-celled organisms gave rise to many-celled organisms, invertebrates gave rise to vertebrates, ape-like creatures gave rise to man, non-intelligent and amoral matter gave rise to intelligence and morality, man's yearnings gave rise to religions, etc.

Professor D.M.S. Watson, one of the leading biologists and science writers of his day, demonstrated the atheistic bias behind much evolutionary thinking when he wrote:

> Evolution [is] a theory universally accepted not because it can be proven by logically coherent evidence to be true, but because the only alternative, special creation, is clearly incredible.[1]

So it's not a question of biased religious creationists versus objective scientific evolutionists; rather, it is the biases of the Christian religion versus the biases of the religion of secular humanism resulting in different interpretations of the same scientific data. As the anti-creationist science writer Boyce Rensberger admits:

> At this point, it is necessary to reveal a little inside information about how scientists work, something the textbooks don't usually

1. D.M.S. Watson, "Adaptation," *Nature*, 124:233, 1929.

tell you. The fact is that scientists are not really as objective and dispassionate in their work as they would like you to think. Most scientists first get their ideas about how the world works not through rigorously logical processes but through hunches and wild guesses. As individuals, they often come to believe something to be true long before they assemble the hard evidence that will convince somebody else that it is. Motivated by faith in his own ideas and a desire for acceptance by his peers, a scientist will labor for years knowing in his heart that his theory is correct but devising experiment after experiment whose results he hopes will support his position.[2]

It's not really a question of who is biased, but which bias is the correct bias with which to be biased! Actually, *Teaching about Evolution* admits in the dialogue on pages 22–25 that science isn't just about facts, and it is tentative, not dogmatic. But the rest of the book is dogmatic that evolution is a fact!

Professor Richard Lewontin, a geneticist (and self-proclaimed Marxist), is a renowned champion of neo-Darwinism, and certainly one of the world's leaders in promoting evolutionary biology. He recently wrote this very revealing comment (the italics were in the original). It illustrates the implicit philosophical bias against Genesis creation — regardless of whether or not the facts support it:

> We take the side of science *in spite* of the patent absurdity of some of its constructs, *in spite* of its failure to fulfil many of its

2. Boyce Rensberger, *How the World Works* (NY: William Morrow 1986), p. 17–18.

extravagant promises of health and life, *in spite* of the tolerance of the scientific community for unsubstantiated just-so stories, because we have a prior commitment, a commitment to materialism. It is not that the methods and institutions of science somehow compel us to accept a material explanation of the phenomenal world, but, on the contrary, that we are forced by our *a priori* adherence to material causes to create an apparatus of investigation and a set of concepts that produce material explanations, no matter how counter-intuitive, no matter how mystifying to the uninitiated. Moreover, that materialism is an absolute, for we cannot allow a Divine Foot in the door.[3]

Many evolutionists chide creationists not because of the facts, but because creationists refuse to play by the current rules of the game that exclude supernatural creation *a priori*.[4] That it is indeed a "game" was proclaimed by the evolutionary biologist Richard Dickerson:

Science is fundamentally a game. It is a game with one overriding and defining rule:

Rule #1: Let us see how far and to what extent we can explain the behavior of the physical and material universe in terms of purely physical and material causes, without invoking the supernatural.[5]

---

3. Richard Lewontin, "Billions and Billions of Demons," *The New York Review*, January 9, 1997, p. 31.

4. C. Wieland, "Science: The Rules of the Game," *Creation Ex Nihilo*, 11(1):47–50, December 1988–February 1989.

5. R.E. Dickerson, *J. Molecular Evolution*, 34:277, 1992; *Perspectives on Science and the Christian Faith*, 44:137–138, 1992.

In practice, the "game" is extended to trying to explain not just the behavior, but the *origin* of everything without the supernatural.

Actually, evolutionists are often not consistent with their own rules against invoking an intelligent designer. For example, when archaeologists find an arrowhead, they can tell it must have been designed, even though they haven't seen the designer. And the whole basis of the SETI program is that a signal from outer space carrying specific information must have an intelligent source. Yet the materialistic bias of many evolutionists means that they reject an intelligent source for the literally encyclopedic information carried in every living cell.

It's no accident that the leaders of evolutionary thought were and are ardently opposed to the notion of the Christian God as revealed in the Bible.[6] Stephen Jay Gould and others have shown that Darwin's purpose was to destroy the idea of a divine designer.[7] Richard Dawkins applauds evolution because he claims that before Darwin it was impossible to be an intellectually fulfilled atheist, as he says he is.[8]

Many atheists have claimed to be atheists precisely because of evolution. For example, the evolutionary entomologist and sociobiologist E.O. Wilson (who has an article in *Teaching about Evolution* on page 15) said:

> As were many persons from Alabama, I
> was a born-again Christian. When I was

6. D. Batten, "A Who's Who of evolutionists," *Creation Ex Nihilo*, 20(1):32, December 1997–February 1998; "How Religiously Neutral Are the Anti-Creationist Organisations?" cited February 18, 1999. Available from the AiG website at <http://www.answersingenesis.org/WebMan/Article.asp?ID=189>.

7. C. Wieland, "Darwin's Real Message: Have You Missed It?" *Creation Ex Nihilo*, 14(4):16–19, September–November 1992.

8. R. Dawkins, *The Blind Watchmaker: Why the Evidence of Evolution Reveals a Universe without Design*, (NY: W.W. Norton, 1986), p. 6.

fifteen, I entered the Southern Baptist Church with great fervor and interest in the fundamentalist religion; I left at seventeen when I got to the University of Alabama and heard about evolutionary theory.[9]

Many people do not realize that the teaching of evolution propagates an anti-biblical religion. The first two tenets of the *Humanist Manifesto II* (1973), signed by many prominent evolutionists, are:

> 1. Religious humanists regard the universe as self-existing and not created.
> 2. Humanism believes that Man is a part of nature and has emerged as a result of a continuous process.

This is exactly what evolution teaches. Many humanist leaders are quite open about using the public schools to proselytize their faith. This might surprise some parents who think the schools are supposed to be free of religious indoctrination, but this quote makes it clear:

> I am convinced that the battle for humankind's future must be waged and won in the *public school classroom* by *teachers* who correctly perceive their role as the *proselytizers of a new faith*: a *religion* of humanity that recognizes and respects the spark of what theologians call divinity in every human being. These teachers must embody the same selfless dedication as the most rabid fundamentalist preachers, for they will be *minis-*

9. E.O. Wilson, *The Humanist*, September/October 1982, p. 40.

ters of another sort, utilizing a classroom instead of a pulpit to *convey humanist values* in *whatever subject they teach*, regardless of the educational level — preschool day care or large state university. The classroom must and will become an arena of conflict between the old and the new — the rotting corpse of Christianity, together with all its adjacent evils and misery, and the *new faith of humanism. . . .*

It will undoubtedly be a long, arduous, painful struggle replete with much sorrow and many tears, but humanism will emerge triumphant. It must if the family of humankind is to survive.[10]

Teaching about Evolution, while claiming to be about science and neutral on religion, has some religious statements of its own. For example on page 6:

To accept the probability of change — and to see change as an agent of opportunity rather than as a threat — is a silent message and challenge in the lesson of evolution.

However, as it admits that evolution is "unpredictable and natural," and has "no specific direction or goal" (p. 127), this message is incoherent.

The authors of *Teaching about Evolution* may realize that the rank atheism of most evolutionary leaders would be repugnant to most American parents if they knew. More recently, the agnostic anti-creationist philosopher Ruse admitted "Evolution as a scientific theory makes a commitment to a kind of naturalism" but this

10. J. Dunphy, "A Religion for a New Age," *The Humanist*, Jan.–Feb. 1983, 23, 26 (emphases added), cited by Wendell R. Bird, *Origin of the Species — Revisited*, vol. 2, p. 257.

"may not be a good thing to admit in a court of law."[11] *Teaching about Evolution* tries to sanitize evolution by claiming that it is compatible with many religions. It even recruits many religious leaders in support. One of the "dialogues" portrays a teacher having much success diffusing opposition by asking the students to ask their pastor, and coming back with "Hey — evolution is okay!" Although the dialogues are fictional, the situation is realistic.

It might surprise many people to realize that many church leaders do not believe their own book, the Bible. This plainly teaches that God created recently in six consecutive normal days, made things to reproduce "after their kind," and that death and suffering resulted from Adam's sin. This is one reason why many Christians regard evolution as incompatible with Christianity. On page 58, *Teaching about Evolution* points out that many religious people believe that "God used evolution" (theistic evolution). But theistic evolution teaches that God used struggle for survival and death, the "last enemy" (1 Cor. 15:26) as His means of achieving a "very good" (Gen. 1:31) creation.[12] Biblical creationists find this objectionable.

The only way to assert that evolution and "religion" are compatible is to regard "religion" as having nothing to do with the real world, and being just subjective. A God who "created" by evolution is, for all practical purposes, indistinguishable from no God at all.

Perhaps *Teaching about Evolution* is letting its guard down sometimes. For example, on page 11 it re-

---

11. Symposium titled "The New Anti-Evolutionism" (during the 1993 annual meeting of the American Association for the Advancement of Science). See C. Wieland, "The Religious Nature of Evolution," *CEN Technical Journal*, 8(1):3–4.

12. W. Gitt, *Did God Use Evolution?* (Bielefeld, Germany: CLV, 1993); D.H. Lane, "A Critique of Theistic Evolution," *Bibliotheca Sacra*, 151:11–31, January–March 1994, Part 1; 151:155-174, April–June 1994, Part 2.

fers to the "explanation provided in Genesis . . . that God created everything in its present form over the course of six days," i.e., Genesis really does teach six-day creation of basic kinds, which contradicts evolution. Therefore, *Teaching about Evolution* is indeed claiming that evolution conflicts with Genesis, and thus with biblical Christianity, although they usually deny that they are attacking "religion." *Teaching about Evolution* often sets up straw men misrepresenting what creationists really do believe. Creationists do not claim that everything was created in exactly the same form as today's creatures. Creationists believe in variation *within a kind*, which is totally different from the *information-gaining* variation required for particles-to-people evolution. This is discussed further in the next chapter.

More blatantly, *Teaching about Evolution* recommends many books that are very openly atheistic, like those by Richard Dawkins (p. 131).[13] On page 129 it says: "Statements about creation . . . should not be regarded as reasonable alternatives to scientific explanations for the origin and evolution of life." Since anything not reasonable is unreasonable, *Teaching about Evolution* is in effect saying that believers in creation are really unreasonable and irrational. This is hardly religiously neutral, but is regarded by many religious people as an attack.

A recent survey published in the leading science journal *Nature* conclusively showed that the National Academy of Sciences, the producers of *Teaching about*

---

13. For refutations of Dawkins' books, see: G.H. Duggan, "Review of *The Blind Watchmaker*," *Apologia*, 6(1):121–122, 1997; K.T. Gallagher, "Dawkins in Biomorph Land," *International Philosophical Quarterly*, 32(4):501–513, December 1992; R.G. Bohlin, "Up the River Without a Paddle — Review of *River Out of Eden: A Darwinian View of Life*," *Creation Ex Nihilo Technical Journal*, 10(3):322–327, 1996; J.D. Sarfati, "Review of *Climbing Mt Improbable*," *Creation Ex Nihilo Technical Journal*, 12(1):29–34, 1998; W. Gitt, "Weasel Words," *Creation Ex Nihilo*, 20(4):20–21, September–November 1998.

Evolution, is heavily biased against God, rather than religiously unbiased.[14] A survey of all 517 NAS members in biological and physical sciences resulted in just over half responding: 72.2 % were overtly atheistic, 20.8 % agnostic, and only 7.0 % believed in a personal God. Belief in God and immortality was lowest among biologists. It is likely that those who didn't respond were unbelievers as well, so the study probably underestimates the level of anti-God belief in the NAS. The percentage of unbelief is far higher than the percentage among U.S. scientists in general, or in the whole U.S. population.

Commenting on the professed religious neutrality of *Teaching about Evolution*, the surveyors comment:

> NAS President Bruce Alberts said: "There are very many outstanding members of this academy who are very religious people, people who believe in evolution, many of them biologists." *Our research suggests otherwise.*[15]

THE BASIS OF MODERN SCIENCE

Many historians, of many different religious persuasions including atheistic, have shown that modern science started to flourish only in largely Christian Europe. For example, Dr. Stanley Jaki has documented how the scientific method was stillborn in all cultures apart from the Judeo-Christian culture of Europe.[16] These historians point out that the basis of modern sci-

14. E.J. Larson and L. Witham, "Leading Scientists Still Reject God," *Nature,* 394(6691):313, July 23, 1998. The sole criterion for being classified as a "leading" or "greater" scientist was membership of the NAS.

15. Ibid., emphasis added.

16. S. Jaki, *Science and Creation* (Edinburgh and London: Scottish Academic Press, 1974).

ence depends on the assumption that the universe was made by a rational creator. An orderly universe makes perfect sense only if it were made by an orderly Creator. But if there is no creator, or if Zeus and his gang were in charge, why should there be any order at all? So, not only is a strong Christian belief not an obstacle to science, such a belief was its very foundation. It is, therefore, fallacious to claim, as many evolutionists do, that believing in miracles means that laboratory science would be impossible. Loren Eiseley stated:

> The philosophy of experimental science . . . began its discoveries and made use of its methods in the faith, not the knowledge, that it was dealing with a rational universe controlled by a creator who did not act upon whim nor interfere with the forces He had set in operation. . . . It is surely one of the curious paradoxes of history that science, which professionally has little to do with faith, owes its origins to an act of faith that the universe can be rationally interpreted, and that science today is sustained by that assumption.[17]

Evolutionists, including Eiseley himself, have thus abandoned the only rational justification for science. But Christians can still claim to have such a justification.

It should thus not be surprising, although it is for many people, that most branches of modern science were founded by believers in *creation*. The list of creationist scientists is impressive.[18] A sample:

---

17. L. Eiseley: *Darwin's Century: Evolution and the Men who Discovered It* (Anchor, NY: Doubleday, 1961).

18. A. Lamont, *21 Great Scientists Who Believed the Bible* (Australia: Creation Science Foundation, 1995), p. 120-131; H.M. Morris, *Men of Science — Men of God* (Green Forest, AR: Master Books, 1982).

Physics	Newton, Faraday, Maxwell, Kelvin
Chemistry	Boyle, Dalton, Ramsay
Biology	Ray, Linnaeus, Mendel, Pasteur, Virchow, Agassiz
Geology	Steno, Woodward, Brewster, Buckland, Cuvier
Astronomy	Copernicus, Galileo, Kepler, Herschel, Maunder
Mathematics	Pascal, Leibnitz, Euler

Even today, many scientists reject particles-to-people evolution (i.e., everything made itself). The Answers in Genesis (Australia) staff scientists have published many scientific papers in their own fields. Dr. Russell Humphreys, a nuclear physicist working with Sandia National Laboratories in Albuquerque, New Mexico, has had over 20 articles published in physics journals, while Dr. John Baumgardner's catastrophic plate tectonics theory was reported in *Nature*. Dr. Edward Boudreaux of the University of New Orleans has published 26 articles and four books in physical chemistry. Dr. Maciej Giertych, head of the Department of Genetics at the Institute of Dendrology of the Polish Academy of Sciences, has published 90 papers in scientific journals. Dr. Raymond Damadian invented the lifesaving medical advance of magnetic resonance imaging (MRI).[19] Dr. Raymond Jones was described as one of Australia's top scientists for his discoveries about

19. J. Mattson and Merrill Simon, *The Pioneers of NMR in Magnetic Resonance in Medicine: The Story of MRI* (Jericho, NY: Bar-Ilan University Press, 1996), chapter 8. See also the interview with Dr. Damadian in *Creation Ex Nihilo*, 16(3):35–37, June–August 1994.

the legume *Leucaena* and bacterial symbiosis with grazing animals, worth millions of dollars per year to Australia.[20] Dr. Brian Stone has won a record number of awards for excellence in engineering teaching at Australian universities.[21] An evolutionist opponent admitted the following about a leading creationist biochemist and debater, Dr. Duane Gish:

> Duane Gish has very strong scientific credentials. As a biochemist, he has synthesized peptides, compounds intermediate between amino acids and proteins. He has been co-author of a number of outstanding publications in peptide chemistry.[22]

A number of highly qualified living creationist scientists can be found on the Answers in Genesis website.[23] So an oft-repeated charge that no real scientist rejects evolution is completely without foundation. Nevertheless, *Teaching about Evolution* claims in this Question and Answer section on page 56:

> Q: Don't many scientists reject evolution?
> A: No. The scientific consensus around evolution is overwhelming. . . .

20. "Standing Firm" [Interview of Raymond Jones with Don Batten and Carl Wieland], *Creation Ex Nihilo,* 21(1):20–22, December 1998–February 1999.

21. "Prize-winning Professor Rejects Evolution: Brian Stone Speaks to Don Batten and Carl Wieland," *Creation Ex Nihilo,* 20(4):52–53, September–November 1998.

22. Sidney W. Fox, *The Emergence of Life: Darwinian Evolution from the Inside* (NY: Basic Books, 1988), p. 46. Fox is a leading chemical evolutionist who believes life evolved from "proteinoid microspheres."

23. Cited February 18, 1999. Available at <http://www.answersingenesis.org /Webman/default.asp?Area=Tools&SubArea=Scientists>.

It is regrettable that *Teaching about Evolution* is not really answering its own question. The actual question should be truthfully answered "Yes," even though evolution-rejecting scientists are in a minority. The explanation for the answer given would be appropriate (even if highly debatable) if the question were: "Is it true that there is no scientific *consensus* around evolution?" But truth is not decided by majority vote!

C.S. Lewis also pointed out that even our ability to reason would be called into question if atheistic evolution were true:

> If the solar system was brought about by an accidental collision, then the appearance of organic life on this planet was also an accident, and the whole evolution of Man was an accident too. If so, then all our thought processes are mere accidents — the accidental by-product of the movement of atoms. And this holds for the materialists' and astronomers' as well as for anyone else's. But if their thoughts — i.e., of Materialism and Astronomy — are merely accidental by-products, why should we believe them to be true? I see no reason for believing that one accident should be able to give a correct account of all the other accidents.[24]

THE LIMITS OF SCIENCE

Science does have its limits. Normal (operational) science deals only with repeatable observable processes in the *present*. This has indeed been very successful in

---

24. C.S. Lewis, *God in the Dock* (Grand Rapids, MI: Wm. B. Eerdmans Publishing Co., 1970), p. 52–53.

understanding the world, and has led to many improvements in the quality of life. In contrast, evolution is a speculation about the unobservable and unrepeatable *past*. Thus the comparison in *Teaching about Evolution* of disbelief in evolution with disbelief in gravity and heliocentrism is highly misleading. It is also wrong to claim that denying evolution is rejecting the type of science that put men on the moon, although many evolutionary propagandists make such claims. (Actually the man behind the Apollo moon mission was the *creationist* rocket scientist Wernher von Braun.[25])

In dealing with the past, "origins science" can enable us to make educated guesses about origins. It uses the principles of causality (everything that has a beginning has a cause[26]) and analogy (e.g., we observe that intelligence is needed to generate complex coded information in the present, so we can reasonably assume the same for the past). But the only way we can be really sure about the past is if we have a reliable eyewitness account. Evolutionists claim there is no such account, so their ideas are derived from assumptions about the past. But biblical creationists believe that Genesis is an eyewitness account of the origin of the universe and living organisms. They also believe that there is good evidence for this claim, so they reject the claim that theirs is a blind faith.[27]

Creationists don't pretend that any knowledge, science included, can be pursued without presuppositions (i.e., prior religious/philosophical beliefs). Creationists affirm that creation cannot ultimately be divorced from the Bible any more than evolution can ultimately be

25. Ann Lamont, *21 Great Scientists who Believed the Bible* (Australia: Creation Science Foundation, 1995), p. 242-251.

26. J.D. Sarfati, "If God Created the Universe, Then Who Created God?" *CEN Technical Journal*, 12(1)20–22, 1998.

divorced from its naturalistic starting point that excludes divine creation *a priori.*

27. Some supporting information can be found in the following works, among others: H.M. Morris with H.M. Morris III, *Many Infallible Proofs* (Green Forest, AR: Master Books, 1996); G.L. Archer, *Encyclopedia of Bible Difficulties* (Grand Rapids, MI: Zondervan, 1982); G.H. Clark, *God's Hammer: The Bible and Its Critics* (Jefferson, MD: The Trinity Foundation, 2nd ed. 1987); P. Enns, *The Moody Handbook of Theology* (Chicago, IL: Moody Press, 1989), chapter 18; N.L. Geisler and R.M. Brooks, *When Skeptics Ask* (Wheaton, IL: Victor Books, 1990); N.L. Geisler and T. R. Howe, *When Critics Ask* (Wheaton, IL: Victor Books, 1992); N.L. Geisler and William E. Nix, *A General Introduction to the Bible* (Chicago, IL: Moody, 1986); H. Lindsell, *The Battle for the Bible* (Grand Rapids, MI: Zondervan, 1976); J. McDowell, *More Evidence That Demands a Verdict* (San Bernardino, CA: Here's Life Publishers, revised ed. 1981); John W. Wenham, *Christ and the Bible* (Guildford, Surrey, UK: Eagle, 3rd ed. 1993).

CHAPTER 2

VARIATION AND NATURAL SELECTION VERSUS EVOLUTION

This chapter contrasts the evolution and creation models, and refutes faulty understandings of both. A major point is the common practice of *Teaching about Evolution and the Nature of Science* to call all change in organisms "evolution." This enables *Teaching about Evolution* to claim that evolution is happening today. However, creationists have never disputed that organisms change; the difference is the *type* of change. A key difference between the two models is whether observed changes are the type to turn particles into people.

EVOLUTION

Evolution, of the fish-to-philosopher type, requires that non-living chemicals organize themselves into a self-reproducing organism. All types of life are alleged to have descended, by natural, ongoing processes, from this "simple" life form. For this to have worked, there must be some process which can generate the genetic information in living things today. Chapter 9 on "Design" shows how encyclopedic this information is.

So how do evolutionists propose that this information arose? The first self-reproducing organism would have made copies of itself. Evolution also requires that the copying is not always completely accurate — errors (mutations) occur. Any mutations which enable an organism to leave more self-reproducing offspring will be passed on through the generations. This "differential reproduction" is called *natural selection*. In summary, evolutionists believe that the source of new genetic information is mutations sorted by natural selection — the neo-Darwinian theory.

CREATION

In contrast, creationists, starting from the Bible, believe that God created different kinds of organisms, which reproduced "after their kinds" (Gen. 1:11–12, 21, 24–25). Each of these kinds was created with a vast amount of information. There was enough variety in the information in the original creatures so their descendants could adapt to a wide variety of environments.

All (sexually reproducing) organisms contain their genetic information in *paired* form. Each offspring inherits half its genetic information from its mother, and half from its father. So there are two genes at a given position (*locus*, plural *loci*) coding for a particular characteristic. An organism can be heterozygous at a given locus, meaning it carries different forms (*alleles*) of this gene. For example, one allele can code for blue eyes, while the other one can code for brown eyes; or one can code for the A blood type and the other for the B type. Sometimes two alleles have a combined effect, while at other times only one allele (called *dominant*) has any effect on the organism, while the other does not (*recessive*).

With humans, both the mother's and father's halves have 100,000 genes, the information equivalent to a thousand 500-page books (3 billion base pairs, as *Teaching about Evolution* correctly states on page 42). The ardent neo-Darwinist Francisco Ayala points out that humans today have an "average heterozygosity of 6.7 percent."[1] This means that for every thousand gene pairs coding for any trait, 67 of the pairs have different alleles, meaning 6,700 heterozygous loci overall. Thus, any single human could produce a vast number of different possible sperm or egg cells — 2^{6700} or 10^{2017}. The number of atoms in the whole known universe is "only" 10^{80}, extremely tiny by comparison. So there is no problem for creationists explaining that the original created kinds could each give rise to many different varieties. In fact, the original created kinds would have had much more heterozygosity than their modern, more specialized descendants. No wonder Ayala pointed out that most of the variation in populations arises from reshuffling of previously existing genes, not from mutations. Many varieties can arise simply by two previously hidden recessive alleles coming together. However, Ayala believes the genetic information came ultimately from mutations, not creation. His belief is contrary to information theory, as shown in chapter 9 on "Design."

DETERIORATION FROM PERFECTION

An important aspect of the creationist model is often overlooked, but it is essential for a proper understanding of the issues. This aspect is the *deterioration* of a once-perfect creation. Creationists believe this because the Bible states that the world was created perfect (Gen. 1:31), and that death and deterioration came into the world because the first human couple sinned

---

1. F.J. Ayala, "The Mechanisms of Evolution," *Scientific American* 239(3):48–61, September 1978, quoted on page 55.

(Gen. 3:19, Rom. 5:12, 8:20–22, 1 Cor. 15:21–22, 26).

As the previous chapter showed, all scientists interpret facts according to their assumptions. From this premise of perfection followed by deterioration, it follows that mutations, as would be expected from copying errors, destroyed some of the original genetic information. Many evolutionists point to allegedly imperfect structures as "proof" of evolution, although this is really an argument against perfect design rather than for evolution. But many allegedly imperfect structures can also be interpreted as a deterioration of once-perfect structures, for example, eyes of blind creatures in caves. However, this fails to explain how sight could have arisen in the first place.[2]

ADAPTATION AND NATURAL SELECTION

Also, the once-perfect environments have deteriorated into harsher ones. Creatures adapted to these new environments, and this adaptation took the form of *weeding out* some genetic information. This is certainly natural selection — evolutionists don't have a monopoly on this. In fact, a creationist, Edward Blyth, thought of the concept 25 years before Darwin's *Origin of Species* was published. But unlike evolutionists, Blyth regarded it as a *conservative* process that would remove defective organisms, thus conserving the health of the population as a whole. Only when coupled with hypothetical information-gaining mutations could natural selection be creative.

For example, the original dog/wolf kind probably had the information for a wide variety of fur lengths. The first animals probably had medium-length fur. In

2. Other alleged imperfections are actually examples of excellent design which was falsely interpreted through ignorance, as an imperfection. A good example is the common claim that the eye is wired backwards, when this is an essential design feature. See "An Eye for Creation: An Interview with Eye-Disease Researcher Dr. George Marshall, University of Glasgow, Scotland," *Creation Ex Nihilo*, 18(4):19–21, 1996; also P.W.V. Gurney, "Our 'Inverted' Retina — Is It Really 'Bad Design'?" *Creation Ex Nihilo*, 13(1):37–44, 1999.

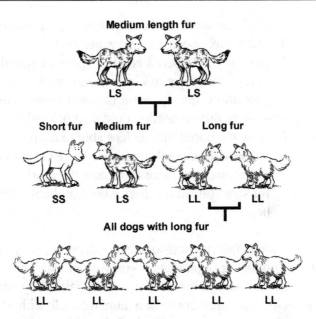

the simplified example illustrated above,[3] a single gene pair is shown under each dog as coming in two possible forms. One form of the gene (L) carries instructions for long fur, the other (S) for short fur.

In row 1, we start with medium-furred animals (LS) interbreeding. Each of the offspring of these dogs can get one of either gene from each parent to make up their two genes.

In row 2, we see that the resultant offspring can have either short (SS), medium (LS) or long (LL) fur. Now imagine the climate cooling drastically (as in the Ice Age). Only those with long fur survive to give rise to the next generation (line 3). So from then on, all the dogs will be a new, long-furred variety. Note that:

1. They are now *adapted* to their environment.
2. They are now more *specialized* than their ancestors on row 1.

3. *Creation* 20(4):31, September–November 1998.

3. This has occurred through *natural selection.*
4. There have been *no new genes* added.
5. In fact, genes have been lost from the population — i.e., there has been *a loss of genetic information,* the opposite of what microbe-to-man evolution needs in order to be credible.
6. Now the population is less able to adapt to future environmental changes — were the climate to become hot, there is no genetic information for short fur, so the dogs would probably overheat.

Another information-losing process occurs in sexually reproducing organisms — remember, each organism inherits only half the information carried by each parent. For example, consider a human couple with only one child, where the mother had the AB blood group (meaning that she has both A and B alleles) and the father had the O blood group (both alleles are O — and recessive). So the child would have either AO or BO alleles, so either the A or the B allele *must* be missing from the child's genetic information. Thus, the child could not have the AB blood group, but would have either the A or the B blood group respectively.[4]

A large population as a whole is less likely to lose established genes because there are usually many copies of the genes of both parents (for example, in their siblings and cousins). But in a small, isolated population, there is a good chance that information can be lost by random sampling. This is called *genetic drift.* Since new mutant genes would start off in small numbers, they are quite likely to be eliminated

4. For information on how creationists can explain the origin of the different human blood groups from a single pair of human ancestors, see J.D. Sarfati, "Blood Types and Their Origin," *Creation Ex Nihilo Technical Journal,* 11(2):31–32, 1997.

by genetic drift, even if they were beneficial.[5]

In an extreme case, where a single pregnant animal or a single pair is isolated, e.g., by being blown or washed onto a desert island, it may lack a number of genes of the original population. So when its descendants fill the island, this new population would be different from the old one, with less information. This is called the *founder effect*.

Loss of information through mutations, natural selection, and genetic drift can sometimes result in different small populations losing such different information that they will no longer interbreed. For example, changes in song or color might result in birds no longer recognizing a mate, so they no longer interbreed. Thus a new "species" is formed.

THE FLOOD

Another aspect of the creationist model is the Bible's teaching in Genesis chapters 6 to 8 that the whole world was flooded, and that a male and female of every kind of land vertebrate (animals with biblical life in the Hebrew *nephesh* sense) were saved on Noah's ark. A few "clean" animals were represented by seven individuals (Gen. 7:2). The Bible also teaches that this ark landed on the mountains of Ararat. From these assumptions, creationists conclude that these kinds multiplied and their descendants spread out over the earth. "Founder effects" would have been common, so many "kinds" would each have given rise to several of today's "species."

---

5. The chance of survival = $2s/(1-e^{-2sN})$, where s = selection coefficient and N is the population size. This asymptotically converges down to $2s$ where sN is large. This means that for a mutation with a selective advantage of 0.1%, considered typical in nature, there is a 99.8% chance that it will be lost. So it is much harder for large populations to substitute beneficial mutations. But smaller populations have their own disadvantages, e.g. they are less likely to produce any good mutations, and are vulnerable to the deleterious effects of inbreeding and genetic drift. See L.M. Spetner, *Not By Chance* (Brooklyn, NY: The Judaica Press, 1996, 1997), chapters 3 and 4.

CONTRASTING THE MODELS

Once biblical creation is properly understood, it is possible to analyze the "evidence" for "evolution as a contemporary process" presented by *Teaching about Evolution* on pages 16–19. The three diagrams below should help:

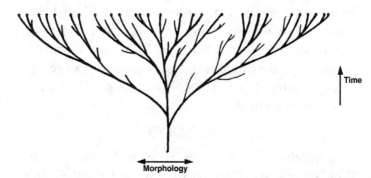

Figure 1: The evolutionary "tree" — which postulates that all today's species are descended from the one common ancestor (which itself evolved from non-living chemicals). This is what evolution is really all about.

Figure 2: The alleged creationist "lawn" — this represents the caricature of creationism presented by Teaching about Evolution — *the Genesis "kinds" were the same as today's species.*

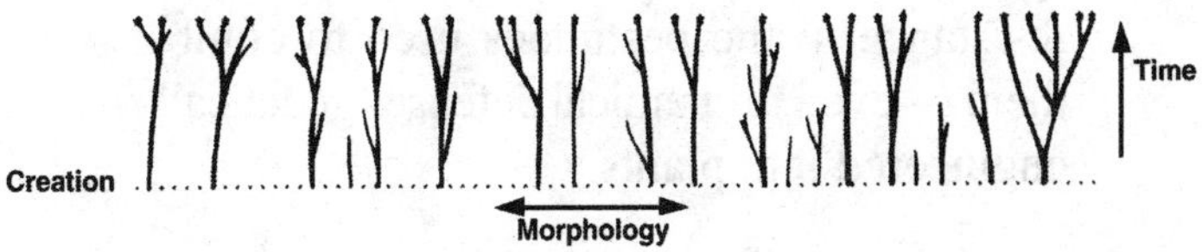

Figure 3: The true creationist "orchard" — diversity has occurred with time within the original Genesis "kinds" (creationists often call them baramin, *from Hebrew* bara = *create, and* min = *kind). Much of the evidence of variation presented by* Teaching about Evolution *refutes only the straw-man version of creationism in Figure 2, but fits the true creationist "orchard" model perfectly well.*

THE ALLEGED EVIDENCE FOR EVOLUTION IN ACTION

This section will deal with some of the examples used by *Teaching about Evolution*, and show that they fit the creationist model better.

ANTIBIOTIC AND PESTICIDE RESISTANCE

Teaching about Evolution claims on pages 16–17:

> The continual evolution of human pathogens has come to pose one of the most serious health problems facing human societies. Many strains of bacteria have become increasingly resistant to antibiotics as natural selection has amplified resistant strains that arose through naturally occurring genetic variation.
>
> Similar episodes of rapid evolution are occurring in many different organisms. Rats have developed resistance to the poison warfarin. Many hundreds of insect species and other agricultural pests have evolved

resistance to the pesticides used to combat them — even to chemical defenses genetically engineered into plants.

However, what has this to do with the evolution of *new kinds* with *new genetic information*? Precisely nothing. What has happened in many cases is that some bacteria *already* had the genes for resistance to the antibiotics. In fact, some bacteria obtained by thawing sources which had been frozen before man developed antibiotics have shown to be antibiotic-resistant. When antibiotics are applied to a population of bacteria, those lacking resistance are killed, and any genetic information they carry is eliminated. The survivors carry less information, but they are all resistant. The same principle applies to rats and insects "evolving" resistance to pesticides. Again, the resistance was already there, and creatures without resistance are eliminated.

In other cases, antibiotic resistance is the result of a mutation, but in all known cases, this mutation has destroyed information. It may seem surprising that destruction of information can sometimes help. But one example is resistance to the antibiotic penicillin. Bacteria normally produce an enzyme, penicillinase, which destroys penicillin. The amount of penicillinase is controlled by a gene. There is normally enough produced to handle any penicillin encountered in the wild, but the bacterium is overwhelmed by the amount given to patients. A mutation disabling this controlling gene results in much more penicillinase being produced. This enables the bacterium to resist the antibiotic. But normally, this mutant would be less fit, as it wastes resources by producing unnecessary penicillinase.

Another example of acquired antibiotic resistance is the transfer of pieces of genetic material (called *plasmids*) between bacteria, even between those of different species. But this is still using *pre-existing* information, and doesn't explain its *origin*.

More information on antibiotic resistance can be found in the article "Superbugs: Not Super after All."[6]

LACEWING SPECIES

Another example of "evolution" is given on page 17, where *Teaching about Evolution* states:

> The North American lacewing species *Chrysoperla carnea* and *Chrysoperla downesi* separated from a common ancestor species recently in evolutionary time and are very similar. But they are different in color, reflecting their different habitats, and they breed at different times of year.

This statement is basically correct, but an evolutionary interpretation of this statement is not the only one possible. A creationist interpretation is that an original *Chrysoperla* kind was created with genes for a wide variety of colors and mating behavior. This has given rise to more specialized descendants. The specialization means that each has lost the information for certain colors and behaviors. The formation of new species (*speciation*) without information gain is no problem for creationists.[7] Adaptation/variation within *Chrysoperla*, which involves no addition of complex new genetic information, says nothing about the origin of lacewings themselves, which is what evolution is supposed to explain.

6. C. Wieland, "Superbugs: Not Super after All," *Creation Ex Nihilo,* 20(1):10–13, June–August 1992.

7. C. Wieland, "Speciation Conference — Good News for Creationists," *Creation Ex Nihilo Technical Journal*, 11(2):136–136, 1997.

DARWIN'S FINCHES

On page 19, *Teaching about Evolution* claims:

A particularly interesting example of contemporary evolution involves the 13 species of finches studied by Darwin on the Galápagos Islands, now known as Darwin's finches. . . . Drought diminishes supplies of easily cracked nuts but permits the survival of plants that produce larger, tougher nuts. Drought thus favors birds with strong, wide beaks that can break these tougher seeds, producing populations of birds with these traits. [Peter and Rosemary Grant of Princeton University] have estimated that if droughts occur about every 10 years on the islands, then a new species of finch might arise in only about 200 years.

However, again, an original population of finches had a wide variety of beak sizes. When a drought occurs, the birds with insufficiently strong and wide beaks can't crack the nuts, so they are eliminated, along with their genetic information. Again, no new information has arisen, so this does not support molecules-to-man evolution.

Also, the rapid speciation (200 years) is good evidence for the biblical creation model. Critics doubt that all of today's species could have fitted on the ark. However, the ark would have needed only about 8,000 kinds of land vertebrate animals, which would be sufficient to produce the wide variety of species we have today.[8]

---

8. J.D. Sarfati, "How Did all the Animals Fit on Noah's Ark?" *Creation Ex Nihilo*, 19(2):16–19, March–May 1997; J. Woodmorappe, *Noah's Ark: A Feasibility Study* (Santee, CA: Institute for Creation Research, 1996).

Darwin's finches show that it need not take very long for new species to arise.[9]

BREEDING VERSUS EVOLUTION

On pages 37–38, *Teaching about Evolution* compares the artificial breeding of pigeons and dogs with evolution. However, all the breeders do is select from the information *already present*. For example, Chihuahuas were bred by selecting the smallest dogs to breed from over many generations. But this process eliminates the genes for large size.

The opposite process would have bred Great Danes from the same ancestral dog population, by eliminating the genes for small size. So the breeding has *sorted out* the information mixture into separate lines. All the breeds have less information than the original dog/wolf kind.

Many breeds are also the victims of hereditary conditions due to mutations, for example the "squashed" snout of the bulldog and pug. But their loss of genetic information and their inherited defects mean that purebred dogs are less "fit" in the wild than mongrels, and veterinarians can confirm that purebreds suffer from more diseases.

Actually, breeds of dogs are interfertile, even Great Danes and Chihuahuas, so they are still the same species. Not that speciation is a problem for creationists — see the section on lacewings above. But if Great Danes and Chihuahuas were only known from the fossil record, they would probably have been classified as different species or even different genera. Indeed, without human

---

9. C. Wieland, "Darwin's Finches: Evidence for Rapid Post-Flood Adaptation," *Creation Ex Nihilo,* 14(3):22–23, June–August 1992; see also C. Wieland, "Review of J. Weiner's Book: *The Beak of the Finch: Evolution in Real Time,*" *CEN Technical Journal,* 9(1):21–24, 1995. The book is full of misleading and patronizing attacks on creationists, and is a major propaganda tool used by *Teaching about Evolution.*

intervention, Great Danes and Chihuahuas could probably not breed together (hybridize), so they could be considered different species in the wild. Creationists regard the breeds of dogs as showing that God programmed much variability into the original dog/wolf created kind.

DARWIN VERSUS A FAULTY CREATION MODEL

On pages 35–36, *Teaching about Evolution* discusses some of Darwin's observations. For example, living and fossil armadillos are found only in South America. Also, animals on the Galápagos Islands are similar to those in Ecuador, while creatures on islands off Africa's coast are related to those in Africa. The book then states:

> Darwin could not see how these observations could be explained by the prevailing view of his time: that each species had been independently created, with the species that were best suited to each location being created at each particular site.

Actually, this is setting up a straw man, as this is not what biblical creationists believe, because it completely ignores the global flood as stated in Genesis chapters 6–9. The flood wiped out all land vertebrates outside the ark and would have totally re-arranged the earth's surface. So, there's no way that anything was created in its present location.

Also, all modern land vertebrates would be descended from those which disembarked from the ark in the mountains of Ararat — over generations, they migrated to their present locations. It should therefore be no surprise to biblical creationists that animals on islands off Africa's coast should be similar to those in Africa — they migrated to the islands via Africa.

Darwin's observations were thus easily explainable by the biblical creation/flood model. However, by Darwin's time, most of his opponents did not believe the biblical creation model, but had "re-interpreted" it to fit into the old-earth beliefs of the day.

A prevalent belief was a series of global floods followed by re-creations, rather than a single flood followed by migration. Darwin found observations which didn't fit this non-biblical model. This then allowed him to discredit creation and the Bible itself, although it wasn't actually the true biblical belief he had disproved!

An interesting experiment by Darwin, cited by *Teaching about Evolution* on page 38, also supports the creation-flood model.

> By floating snails on salt water for prolonged periods, Darwin convinced himself that, on rare occasions, snails might have "floated in chunks of drifted timber across moderately wide arms of the sea." . . . Prior to Darwin, the existence of land snails and bats, but not typical terrestrial mammals, on the oceanic islands was simply noted and catalogued as a fact. It is unlikely that anyone would have thought to test the snails for their ability to survive for prolonged periods in salt water. Even if they had, such an experiment would have had little impact.

Thus, Darwin helped answer a problem raised by skeptics of the Bible and its account of the flood and ark: "How did the animals get to faraway places?" This also showed that some invertebrates could have survived the flood outside the ark,[10] possibly on rafts of pumice or tangled vegetation, or on driftwood as Darwin suggested. Other experiments by Darwin showed that garden seeds could still sprout after 42 days' immersion in salt water, so they could have traveled 1,400 miles (2,240 km) on a typical ocean current.[11] This shows how plants could have survived without being on the ark — again by floating on driftwood, pumice, or vegetation rafts — even if they were often soaked. Therefore, the creation-flood-migration model could also have led to such experiments, despite what *Teaching about Evolution* implies.[12]

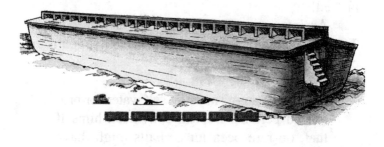

10. Creationists, starting from the Bible, point out that the Hebrew words for the animals taken on the ark do not include invertebrates, and believe that invertebrates probably do not have life in the *nephesh* sense. From these premises, it follows that they must have survived off the ark somehow. For some plausible solutions to this and other problems people have raised about the ark, see reference 8.

11. J. Weiner, *The Beak of the Finch: Evolution in Real Time* (London: Random House), page 136.

12. As for questions like "How Did Koalas Get to Australia?" there are several possibilities. Land vertebrates could have migrated widely when land bridges were exposed when the sea level was lower during the post-flood Ice Age. Another important factor is introduction by humans. That's how the rabbit reached Australia, and some of Australia's animals could have arrived with the Aborigines. See *The Answers Book* by Ken Ham, Andrew Snelling, and Carl Wieland (Green Forest, AR: Master Books, Inc., 1993).

CHAPTER 3

THE LINKS ARE MISSING

*T*eaching about Evolution and the Nature of Science discusses the fossil record in several places. Creationists and evolutionists, with their different assumptions, predict different things about the fossil record. If living things had really evolved from other kinds of creatures, then there would have been many intermediate or transitional forms, with halfway structures. However, if different kinds had been created separately, the fossil record should show creatures appearing abruptly and fully formed.

THE TRANSITIONAL FOSSILS PROBLEM

Charles Darwin was worried that the fossil record did not show what his theory predicted:

> Why is not every geological formation and every stratum full of such intermediate links? Geology assuredly does not reveal any such finely graduated organic chain; and this is the most obvious and serious objection which can be urged against the theory.[1]

---

1. C.R. Darwin, *Origin of Species*, 6th edition, 1872 (London: John Murray, 1902), p. 413.

Is it any different today? The late Dr. Colin Patterson, senior paleontologist of the British Museum of Natural History, wrote a book, *Evolution*. In reply to a questioner who asked why he had not included any pictures of transitional forms, he wrote:

> I fully agree with your comments about the lack of direct illustration of evolutionary transitions in my book. If I knew of any, fossil or living, I would certainly have included them. . . . I will lay it on the line — there is not one such fossil for which one could make a watertight argument.[2]

The renowned evolutionist (and Marxist) Stephen Jay Gould wrote:

> The absence of fossil evidence for intermediary stages between major transitions in organic design, indeed our inability, even in our imagination, to construct functional intermediates in many cases, has been a persistent and nagging problem for gradualistic accounts of evolution.[3]

And:

> I regard the failure to find a clear "vec-

---

2. C. Patterson, letter to Luther D. Sunderland, April 10, 1979, as published in *Darwin's Enigma* (Green Forest, AR: Master Books, 4th ed. 1988), p. 89. Patterson later tried to backtrack somewhat from this clear statement, apparently alarmed that creationists would utilize this truth.

3. S.J. Gould, in *Evolution Now: A Century After Darwin*, ed. John Maynard Smith, (New York: Macmillan Publishing Co., 1982), p. 140. *Teaching about Evolution* pages 56–57 publishes a complaint by Gould about creationists quoting him about the rarity of transitional forms. He accuses creationists of representing him as denying evolution itself. This complaint is unjustified. Creationists make it very clear that he is a staunch evolutionist — the whole point is that he is a "hostile witness."

tor of progress" in life's history as the most puzzling fact of the fossil record.[4]

As Sunderland points out:

> It of course would be no puzzle at all if he [Gould] had not decided before he examined the evidence that common-ancestry evolution was a fact, "like apples falling from a tree," and that we can only permit ourselves to discuss possible mechanisms to explain that assumed fact.[5]

THE GAPS ARE HUGE

Teaching about Evolution avoids discussing the vast gulf between non-living matter and the first living cell, single-celled and multicelled creatures, and invertebrates and vertebrates. The gaps between these groups should be enough to show that molecules-to-man evolution is without foundation.

There are many other examples of different organisms appearing abruptly and fully formed in the fossil record. For example, the first bats, pterosaurs, and birds were fully fledged flyers. The photograph on the following page shows that bats have always been bats.[6]

Turtles are a well designed and specialized group of reptiles, with a distinctive shell protecting the body's vital organs. However, evolutionists admit "Intermediates between turtles and cotylosaurs, the primitive reptiles from which [evolutionists believe] turtles probably sprang, are entirely lacking." They can't plead an incomplete fossil record because "turtles leave more and better fossil

---

4. S.J. Gould, "The Ediacaran Experiment," *Natural History,* 93(2):14–23, Feb. 1984.

5. L. Sunderland, ref. 2, p. 47–48.

6. Photograph and information courtesy of Dr. Joachim Scheven of the Lebendige Vorwelt Museum in Germany.

remains than do other vertebrates."[7] The "oldest known sea turtle" was a fully formed turtle, not at all transitional. It had a fully developed system for excreting salt, without which a marine reptile would quickly dehydrate. This is shown by skull cavities which would have held large salt-excreting glands around the eyes.[8]

Above right: Palaeochiropteryx tupaiodon — *one of the "oldest" (by evolutionary reckoning) fossil bats. It was found in the Messel oil shale pit near Darmstadt, Germany, and is "dated" between 48 and 54 million years old. It clearly had fully developed wings, and its inner ear had the same construction as those of modern bats, showing that it had full sonar equipment (see chapter 9 for more details of this exquisitely designed system).*
Above left: Artist's impression of a living horseshoe bat.[9]

7. "Reptiles," *Encyclopedia Britannica,* 26:704–705, 15th ed., 1992.

8. Ren Hirayama, "Oldest Known Sea Turtle," *Nature,* 392(6678):705–708, April 16, 1998; comment by Henry Gee, p. 651, same issue.

9. Courtesy of Steve Cardno, 1998.

All 32 mammal orders appear abruptly and fully formed in the fossil record. The evolutionist paleontologist George Gaylord Simpson wrote in 1944:

> The earliest and most primitive members of every order already have the basic ordinal characters, and in no case is an approximately continuous series from one order to another known. In most cases the break is so sharp and the gap so large that the origin of the order is speculative and much disputed.[10]

There is little to overturn that today.[11]

EXCUSES

Like most evolutionary propaganda, *Teaching about Evolution* makes assertions that there are many transitional forms, and gives a few "examples." A box on page 15 contains the gleeful article by the evolutionist (and atheist) E.O. Wilson, "Discovery of a Missing Link." He claimed to have studied "nearly exact intermediates between solitary wasps and the highly social modern ants." But another atheistic evolutionist, W.B. Provine, says that Wilson's "assertions are explicitly denied by the text. . . . Wilson's comments are misleading at best."[12]

Teaching about Evolution emphasizes *Archaeopteryx* and an alleged land mammal-to-whale transition series, so they are covered in chapters 4 and 5 of this

---

10. G.G. Simpson, *Tempo and Mode in Evolution* (NY: Columbia University Press, 1944), p. 105–106.

11. A useful book on the fossil record is D.T. Gish, *Evolution: The Fossils STILL Say NO!* (El Cahon, CA: Institute for Creation Research, 1995).

12. *"Teaching about Evolution and the Nature of Science,* A Review by Dr. Will B. Provine." Available from http://fp.bio.utk.edu/darwin/NAS_guidebook/provine_1.html, at February 18, 1999.

book. *Teaching about Evolution* also makes the following excuse on page 57:

> Some changes in populations might occur too rapidly to leave many transitional fossils. Also, many organisms were very unlikely to leave fossils because of their habitats or because they had no body parts that could easily be fossilized.

Darwin also excused the lack of transitional fossils by "the extreme imperfection of the fossil record." But as we have seen, even organisms that leave excellent fossils, like turtles, are lacking in intermediates. Michael Denton points out that 97.7 percent of living orders of land vertebrates are represented as fossils and 79.1 percent of living families of land vertebrates — 87.8 percent if birds are excluded, as they are less likely to become fossilized.[13]

It's true that fossilization requires specific conditions. Normally, when a fish dies, it floats to the top and rots and is eaten by scavengers. Even if some parts reach the bottom, the scavengers take care of them. Scuba divers don't find the sea floor covered with dead animals being slowly fossilized. The same applies to land animals. Millions of buffaloes (bison) were killed in North America last century, but there are very few fossils.

In nature, a well-preserved fossil generally requires rapid burial (so scavengers don't obliterate the carcass), and cementing agents to harden the fossil quickly. *Teaching about Evolution* has some good photos of a fossil fish with well-preserved features (p. 3) and a jellyfish (p. 36). Such fossils certainly could not have formed

---

13. M. Denton, *Evolution, a Theory in Crisis* (Chevy Chase, MD: Adler & Adler, 1985), p. 190.

gradually — how long do dead jellyfish normally retain their features? If you wanted to form such fossils, the best way might be to dump a load of concrete on top of the creature! Only catastrophic conditions can explain most fossils — for example, a global flood and its aftermath of widespread regional catastrophism.

Teaching about Evolution goes on to assert after the previous quote:

> However, in many cases, such as between primitive fish and amphibians, amphibians and reptiles, reptiles and mammals, and reptiles and birds, there are excellent transitional fossils.

But *Teaching about Evolution* provides no evidence for this! We can briefly examine some of the usual evolutionary claims below (for reptile-to-bird, see the next chapter on birds):

- *Fish to amphibian:* Some evolutionists believe that amphibians evolved from a Rhipidistian fish, something like the coelacanth. It was believed that they used their fleshy, lobed fins for walking on the sea-floor before emerging on the land. This speculation seemed impossible to disprove, since according to evolutionary/long-age interpretations of the fossil record, the last coelacanth lived about 70 million years ago. But a living coelacanth (*Latimeria chalumnae*) was discovered in 1938. And it was found that the fins were not used for walking but for deft maneuvering when swimming. Its soft parts were also totally fish-like, not transitional. It also has some unique features — it gives birth to live young after about a year's gestation, it has a small second tail to help its swimming, and a gland that detects electrical signals.[14] The earliest amphibian, *Ichthyostega* (mentioned on p. 39 of *Teaching about Evolution*), is hardly transitional, but has fully formed legs and shoulder and pelvic girdles, while there is no trace of these in the Rhipidistians.

- *Amphibian to reptile: Seymouria* is a commonly touted intermediate between amphibians and reptiles. But this creature is dated (by evolutionary dating methods) at 280 million years ago, about 30 million years *younger* than the "earliest" true reptiles *Hylonomus* and *Paleothyris*. That is, reptiles are allegedly millions of years older than their alleged ancestors! Also, there is no good reason for thinking it was not completely amphibian in its reproduction. The jump from amphibian to reptile eggs requires the development of a number of new structures and a change in biochemistry — see the section below on soft part changes.

- *Reptile to mammal:* The "mammal-like reptiles" are commonly asserted to be transitional. But according to a specialist on these creatures:

> Each species of mammal-like reptile that has been found appears suddenly in the fossil record and is not preceded by the species that is directly ancestral to it. It disappears some time later, equally abruptly, without leaving a directly descended species.[15]

Evolutionists believe that the earbones of mammals evolved from some jawbones of reptiles. But

---

14. M. Denton, footnote 13, p. 157, 178–180; see also W. Roush, " 'Living Fossil' Is Dethroned," *Science,* 277(5331):1436, September 5, 1997, and "No Stinking Fish in My Tail," *Discover,* March 1985, p. 40.

15. T.S. Kemp, "The Reptiles that Became Mammals," *New Scientist,* 92:583, March 4, 1982.

Patterson recognized that there was no clear-cut connection between the jawbones of "mammal-like reptiles" and the earbones of mammals. In fact, evolutionists have argued about which bones relate to which.[16]

THE FUNCTION OF POSSIBLE INTERMEDIATES

The inability to imagine functional intermediates is a real problem. If a bat or bird evolved from a land animal, the transitional forms would have forelimbs that were neither good legs nor good wings. So how would such things be selected? The fragile long limbs of hypothetical halfway stages of bats and pterosaurs would seem more like a hindrance than a help.

SOFT PART CHANGES

Of course, the soft parts of many creatures would also have needed to change drastically, and there is little chance of preserving them in the fossil record. For example, the development of the amniotic egg would have required many different innovations, including:

- The shell.
- The two new membranes — the amnion and allantois.
- Excretion of water-insoluble uric acid rather than urea (urea would poison the embryo).
- Albumen together with a special acid to yield its water.
- Yolk for food.
- A change in the genital system allowing the fertilization of the egg before the shell hardens.[17]

---

16. C. Patterson, "Morphological Characters and Homology;" in K.A. Joysey and A.E. Friday (eds.), *Problems of Phylogenetic Reconstruction*, Proceedings of an International Symposium held in Cambridge, The Systematics Association Special Volume 21 (Academic Press, 1982), 21–74.

17. M. Denton, footnote 13, p. 218–219.

Another example is the mammals — they have many soft-part differences from reptiles, for example:

- Mammals have a different circulatory system, including red blood cells without nuclei, a heart with four chambers instead of three and one aorta instead of two, and a fundamentally different system of blood supply to the eye.
- Mammals produce milk, to feed their young.
- Mammalian skin has two extra layers, hair and sweat glands.
- Mammals have a diaphragm, a fibrous, muscular partition between the thorax and abdomen, which is vital for breathing. Reptiles breathe in a different way.
- Mammals keep their body temperature constant (warm-bloodedness), requiring a complex temperature control mechanism.
- The mammalian ear has the complex organ of Corti, absent from all reptile ears.[18]
- Mammalian kidneys have a "very high ultrafiltration rate of the blood." This means the heart must be able to produce the required high blood pressure. Mammalian kidneys excrete urea instead of uric acid, which requires different chemistry. They are also finely regulated to maintain constant levels of substances in the blood, which requires a complex endocrine system.[19]

---

18. D. Dewar, *The Transformist Illusion*, 2nd edition, (Ghent, NY: Sophia Perennis et Universalis, 1995), p. 223–232.

19. T.S. Kemp, *Mammal-like Reptiles and the Origin of Mammals* (New York: Academic Press, 1982), p. 309–310.

CHAPTER 4

BIRD EVOLUTION?

B irds are animals with unique features like feathers and special lungs, and most are well designed for flight. Evolutionists believe they evolved from reptiles, maybe even a type of dinosaur. *Teaching about Evolution and the Nature of Science* even presents an alleged dinosaur-bird intermediate as evidence for evolution. This intermediate and other arguments for bird evolution are critically examined in this chapter. This chapter also provides detailed information on some of the unique features of birds.

ARCHAEOPTERYX

Teaching about Evolution has several imaginary "dialogues" between teachers. In one of them (p.8), there is the following exchange:

> *Karen:* A student in one of my classes at the university told me that there are big gaps in the fossil record. Do you know anything about that?
>
> *Doug:* Well, there's *Archaeopteryx*. It's a fossil that has feathers like a bird but the skeleton of a small dinosaur. It's one of those missing links that's not missing any more.

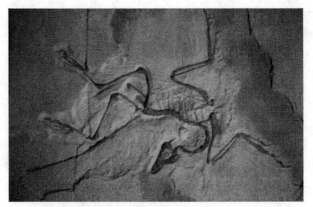

Teaching about Evolution *pictured an* Archaeopteryx *fossil like this one.*

On the same page, there is a picture of a fossil of *Archaeopteryx*, stating:

> A bird that lived 150 million years ago and had many reptilian characteristics, was discovered in 1861 and helped support the hypothesis of evolution proposed by Charles Darwin in *The Origin of Species* two years earlier.

However, Alan Feduccia, a world authority on birds at the University of North Carolina at Chapel Hill and an evolutionist himself, disagrees with assertions like those of "Doug:"

> Paleontologists have tried to turn *Archaeopteryx* into an earth-bound, feathered dinosaur. But it's not. It is a bird, a perching bird. And no amount of "paleobabble" is going to change that.[1]

---

1. Cited in V. Morell, "*Archaeopteryx*: Early Bird Catches a Can of Worms," *Science,* 259(5096):764–65, February 5, 1993.

A legitimate artist's reconstruction of Archaeopteryx, *consistent with its known bird features.*[2]

Archaeopteryx had fully formed flying feathers (including asymmetric vanes and ventral, reinforcing furrows as in modern flying birds), the classical elliptical wings of modern woodland birds, and a large wishbone for attachment of muscles responsible for the downstroke of the wings.[3] Its brain was essentially that of a flying bird, with a large cerebellum and visual cortex. The fact that it had teeth is irrelevant to its alleged transitional status — a number of extinct birds had teeth, while many reptiles do not. Furthermore, like other birds, both its maxilla (upper jaw) and mandible (lower jaw) moved. In most vertebrates, including reptiles, only the mandible moves.[4]

2. Courtesy of Steve Cardno, 1994.

3. A. Feduccia, "Evidence from Claw Geometry Indicating Arboreal Habits of *Archaeopteryx*," *Science,* 259(5096):790–793, February 5, 1993.

4. D. Menton and C. Wieland, "Bird Evolution Flies Out the Window," *Creation Ex Nihilo,* 16(4):16–19, September–November 1994.

FEATHERED DINOSAURS?

In the last few years, the media have run headlines about alleged "feathered dinosaurs" proving that dinosaurs evolved into birds. These alleged ancestors are types of *theropods*, the group of carnivorous dinosaurs that includes *Tyrannosaurus rex*.

We should remember that the media often sensationalize "proofs" of evolution, but the later disproofs, even by other evolutionists, hardly rate a mention. For example, in 1996 there were headlines like "Feathered Fossil Proves Some Dinosaurs Evolved into Birds."[5] This was about a fossil called *Sinosauropteryx prima*.[6] Creationist publications advised readers to be skeptical and keep an open mind.[7] They were vindicated when four leading paleontologists, including Yale University's John Ostrom, later found that the "feathers" were just a parallel array of fibres,[8] probably collagen.

Another famous alleged dino-bird link was *Mononykus*, claimed to be a "flightless bird."[9] The cover of *Time* magazine even illustrated it with feathers, although not the slightest trace of feathers had been found.[10] Later evidence indicated that "*Mononykus* was clearly not a bird . . . it clearly was a fleet-footed fossorial [digging] theropod."[11]

---

5. *The Examiner,* Launceston, Tasmania, October 19, 1996.

6. Ann Gibbons, "New Feathered Fossil Brings Dinosaurs and Birds Closer," *Science,* 274:720–721, 1996.

7. J.D. Sarfati, "Kentucky Fried Dinosaur?" *Creation Ex Nihilo,* 19(2):6, March–May 1997.

8. *New Scientist,* 154(2077):13, April 12, 1997; *Creation,* 19(3):6, June–August 1997.

9. A. Perle et al., "Flightless Bird from the Cretaceous of Mongolia," *Nature,* 362:623–626, 1993; note correction of the name to *Mononykus,* as Perle et al.'s choice, *Mononychus,* was already taken, *Nature,* 363:188, 1993.

10. *Time* (Australia), April 26, 1993.

11. D.P. Prothero and R.M. Schoch, editors, *Major Features of Vertebrate Evolution*, "On the Origin of Birds and of Avian Flight," by J.H. Ostrom (Knoxville, TN: University of Tennessee Press, 1994), p. 160–177.

Many news agencies have reported (June 1998) on two fossils found in Northern China that are claimed to be feathered theropods (meat-eating dinosaurs). The fossils, *Protarchaeopteryx robusta* and *Caudipteryx zoui*, are claimed to be "the immediate ancestors of the first birds."[12]

The two latest discoveries are "dated" at 120 to 136 million years while *Archaeopteryx*, a true bird, is "dated" at 140 to 150 million years, making these "bird ancestors" far younger than their descendants!

Feduccia is not convinced, and neither is his colleague, University of Kansas paleontologist Larry Martin. Martin says: "You have to put this into perspective. To the people who wrote the paper, the chicken would be a feathered dinosaur."[13] Feduccia and Martin believe that *Protarchaeopteryx* and *Caudipteryx* are more likely to be flightless birds similar to ostriches. They have bird-like teeth and lack the long tail seen in theropods. *Caudipteryx* even used gizzard stones like modern plant-eating birds, but unlike theropods.[14]

There are many problems with the dinosaur-to-bird dogma. Feduccia points out:

> "It's biophysically impossible to evolve flight from such large bipeds with foreshortened forelimbs and heavy, balancing tails," exactly the wrong anatomy for flight.[15]

There is also very strong evidence from the forelimb structures that dinosaurs could not have been the

---

12. Ji Qiang, P.J. Currie, M.A. Norell, and Ji Shu-An, "Two Feathered Dinosaurs from Northeastern China," *Nature,* 393(6687):753–761, June 25, 1998. Perspective by K. Padian, same issue, p. 729–730.

13. Cited June 24, 1998, CNN website <http://www.cnn.com/>.

14. *Washington Post,* June 25, 1998.

15. A. Gibbons, "New Feathered Fossil Brings Dinosaurs and Birds Closer," *Science,* 274:720–721, 1996.

ancestors of birds. A team led by Feduccia studied bird embryos under a microscope, and published their study in the journal *Science*.[16] Their findings were reported as follows:

> New research shows that birds lack the embryonic thumb that dinosaurs had, suggesting that it is "almost impossible" for the species to be closely related.[17]

DID GLIDERS TURN INTO FLIERS?

Feduccia and Martin reject the idea that birds evolved from dinosaurs, with good reason. But they are unwilling to abandon evolution, so instead they believe that birds evolved from reptiles called *crocodilomorphs*. They propose these small, crocodile-like reptiles lived in trees, and "initially leapt, then glided from perch to perch."[18]

But a gliding stage is *not* intermediate between a land animal and a flier. Gliders either have even longer wings than fliers (compare a glider's wingspan with an airplane's, or the wingspan of birds like the albatross which spend much time gliding), or have a wide membrane which is quite different from a wing (note the shape of a hang-glider or a flying squirrel). Flapping flight also requires highly controlled muscle movements to achieve flight, which in turn requires that the brain has the program for these movements. Ultimately, this

---

16. A.C. Burke and A. Feduccia, "Developmental Patterns and the Identification of Homologies in the Avian Hand," *Science,* 278(5338):666–8, October 24, 1997, with a perspective by R. Hinchliffe, "The Forward March of the Bird-Dinosaurs Halted?" p. 596–597; J.D. Sarfati, "Dino-Bird Evolution Falls Flat," *Creation,* 20(2):41, March 1998.

17. *The Cincinnati Enquirer,* October 25, 1997.

18. P. Shipman, "Birds Do It . . . Did Dinosaurs?" *New Scientist,* 153(2067):26–31, February 1, 1997, p. 28.

requires new genetic information that a non-flying creature lacks.

Another problem is:

> Neither their hypothetical ancestor nor transitional forms linking it to known fossil birds have been found. And although they rightly argue that cladistic analyses [comparisons of shared characteristics] are only as good as the data upon which they are based, no cladistic study has yet suggested a non-theropod ancestor.[19]

In short, Feduccia and Martin provide devastating criticism against the idea that birds evolved "ground up" from running dinosaurs (the *cursorial* theory). But the dino-to-bird advocates counter with equally powerful arguments against Feduccia and Martin's "trees-down" (*arboreal*) theory. The evidence indicates that the critics are both right — birds did not evolve either from running dinos or from tree-living mini-crocodiles. In fact, birds did not evolve from non-birds at all! This is consistent with the biblical account that distinct kinds of birds were created on Day 5 (Gen. 1:20–23).

THE DIFFERENCES BETWEEN REPTILES AND BIRDS

All evolutionists believe that birds evolved from some sort of reptile, even if they can't agree on the kind. However, reptiles and birds are very different in many ways. Flying birds have streamlined bodies, with the weight centralized for balance in flight; hollow bones for lightness which are also part of their breathing system; powerful muscles for flight, with specially designed long tendons that run over pulley-like openings in the

---

19. Ibid.

shoulder bones; and very sharp vision. And birds have two of the most brilliantly designed structures in nature — their feathers and special lungs.

FEATHERS

Feduccia says "Feathers are a near-perfect adaptation for flight" because they are lightweight, strong,

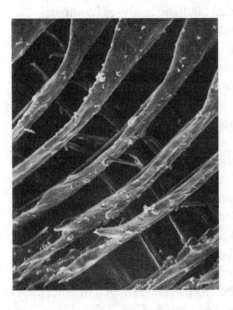

aerodynamically shaped, and have an intricate structure of barbs and hooks. This structure makes them waterproof, and a quick preen with the bill will cause flattened feathers to snap into fully aerodynamic shape again.[20]

Examine the amazing close-up (left) of the barbules of a feather showing the tiny hooklets and grooves (magnified 20,000 times).[21]

The atheistic evolutionist Richard Dawkins, in a book highly recommended by *Teaching about Evolution,* glibly states: *"Feathers are modified reptilian scales,"*[22] a widely held view among evolutionists. But scales are folds in skin; feathers are complex structures

---

20. A. Feduccia, *The Origin and Evolution of Birds* (New Haven, CT: Yale University Press, 1996), p. 130.

21. Photo courtesy of Dr. David Menton.

22. R. Dawkins, *Climbing Mount Improbable* (Harmondsworth, Middlesex, England: Penguin Books, 1996), p. 113.

Photos courtesy of Dr. David Menton.

See the contrast here between the detailed structures of a feather (upper) and scales (lower), both magnified 80 times.

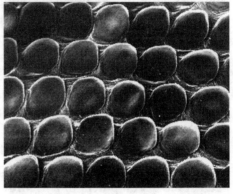

with a barb, barbules, and hooks. They also originate in a totally different way, from follicles inside the skin in a manner akin to hair.

In chapter 2 we showed that every structure or organ must be represented by *information* at the genetic level, written in a chemical alphabet on the long molecule DNA. Clearly, the information required to code for the construction of a feather is of a substantially different order from that required for a scale. For scales to have evolved into feathers means that a significant amount of genetic information had to arise in the bird's DNA which was not present in that of its alleged reptile ancestor.

As usual, natural selection would not favor the hypothetical intermediate forms. Many evolutionists claim that dinosaurs developed feathers for insulation and later evolved and refined them for flight purposes. But like all such "just-so" stories, this fails to explain *how* the new genetic information arose so it could be selected for.

Another problem is that selection for heat insulation is *quite different* from selection for flight. On birds that have lost the ability to fly, the feathers have also lost much of their structure and become hair-like. On flightless birds, mutations degenerating the aerodynamic feather structure would not be as much a handicap as they would be on a flying bird. Therefore, natural selection would not eliminate them, and might even select *for* such degeneration. As usual, loss of flight and feather structure are *losses of information*, so are irrelevant to evolution, which requires an *increase* of information. All that matters is that the feathers provide insulation, and hair-like structures are fine — they work for mammals.[23] That is, natural selection would work against the development of a *flight* feather if the feathers were needed for insulation. And hairy feathers are adequate.

Downy feathers are also good insulators and are common on flightless birds. Their fluffiness is because they *lack the hooks* of flight feathers. Again, natural selection would work to *prevent* evolution of aerodynamic feathers from heat insulators.

Finally, feather proteins (ϕ-keratins) are biochemically different from skin and scale proteins (α-keratins), as well. One researcher concluded:

> At the morphological level feathers are traditionally considered homologous with reptilian scales. However, in development, mor-

23. A. Feduccia, *The Origin and Evolution of Birds* (New Haven, CT: Yale University Press, 1996), p. 130.

phogenesis [shape/form generation], gene structure, protein shape and sequence, and filament formation and structure, feathers are different.[24]

THE AVIAN LUNG

Drastic changes are needed to turn a reptile lung into a bird lung. In reptile lungs, the air is drawn into tiny sacs (*alveoli*, singular *alveolus*) where blood extracts the oxygen and releases carbon dioxide. The stale air is then breathed out the same way it came in. But birds have a complicated system of air sacs, even involving the hollow bones. This system keeps air flowing in one direction through special tubes (*parabronchi*, singular *parabronchus*) in the lung, and blood moves through the lung's blood vessels in the opposite direction for efficient oxygen uptake,[25] an excellent engineering design.[26]

How would the "bellows"-style lungs of reptiles evolve gradually into avian lungs? The hypothetical intermediate stages could not conceivably function properly, meaning the poor animal would be unable to breathe. So natural selection would work to preserve the existing arrangement, by eliminating any misfit intermediates.

Also, even assuming that we could construct a theoretical series of functional intermediate stages, would natural selection "drive" the changes? Probably not —

24. A.H. Brush, "On the Origin of Feathers," *Journal of Evolutionary Biology*, 9:131-142, 1996.

25. M. Denton, *Evolution, a Theory in Crisis* (Bethesda, MD: Adler & Adler, 1985), p. 199-213; K. Schmidt-Nielsen, "How Birds Breathe," *Scientific American*, December 1971, p. 72-79.

26. Engineers make much use of this *principle of counter-current exchange* which is common in living organisms as well — see P.F. Scholander, "The Wonderful Net," *Scientific American*, April 1957, p. 96–107.

bats manage perfectly well with bellows-style lungs — some can even hunt at an altitude of over two miles (three km). The avian lung, with its super-efficiency, becomes especially advantageous only at very high altitudes with low oxygen levels. There would thus have been no selective advantage in replacing the reptilian lung.[27]

We should probably not be surprised that Alan Feduccia's major work on bird evolution doesn't even touch this problem.[28]

Some recent researchers of *Sinosauropteryx*'s lung structure showed that "its bellows-like lungs could not have evolved into high performance lungs of modern birds."[29]

Interestingly, some defenders of dinosaur-to-bird evolution discount this evidence against their theory by saying, "The proponents of this argument offer no animal whose lungs could have given rise to those in birds, which are extremely complex and are unlike the lungs of any living animal."[30] Of course, only evolutionary faith requires that bird lungs arose from lungs of another animal.

27. Michael Denton, "Blown Away By Design," *Creation Ex Nihilo Technical Journal,* 21(4):14–15.

28. A. Feduccia, *The Origin and Evolution of Birds* (New Haven, CT: Yale University Press, 1996). However, this book shows that the usual dinosaur-to-bird dogma has many holes.

29. Ann Gibbons, "New Feathered Fossil Brings Dinosaurs and Birds Closer," *Science,* 274:720–721, 1996.

30. K. Padian and L.M. Chiappe, "The Origin of Birds and Their Flight," *Scientific American,* 278(2), 38–47, February 1998, p. 43.

CHAPTER 5

WHALE EVOLUTION?

etaceans (whales and dolphins) are actually mammals, not fish. But they live their whole lives in water, unlike most mammals that live on land. But evolutionists believe that cetaceans evolved from land mammals. One alleged transitional series is prominently drawn in *Teaching about Evolution and the Nature of Science*. This chapter analyzes this and other arguments for cetacean evolution, and shows some of the unique features of whales and dolphins.

WONDERFUL WHALES

Cetaceans have many unique features to enable them to live in water. For example:

- Enormous lung capacity with efficient oxygen exchange for long dives.
- A powerful tail with large horizontal flukes enabling very strong swimming.
- Eyes designed to see properly in water with its far higher refractive index, and withstand high pressure.
- Ears designed differently from those of land mammals that pick up airborne sound waves and with the eardrum protected from high pressure.

- Skin lacking hair and sweat glands but incorporating fibrous, fatty blubber.
- Whale fins and tongues have counter-current heat exchangers to minimize heat loss.
- Nostrils on the top of the head (blowholes).
- Specially fitting mouth and nipples so the baby can be breast-fed underwater.
- Baleen whales have sheets of baleen (whalebone) that hang from the roof of the mouth and filter plankton for food.

Many cetaceans find objects by echo-location. They have a sonar system which is so precise that it's the envy of the U.S. Navy. It can detect a fish the size of a golf ball 230 feet (70 m) away. It took an expert in chaos theory to show that the dolphin's "click" pattern is mathematically designed to give the best information.[1]

One amazing adaptation of most echo-locating dolphins and small whales is the "melon," a fatty protrusion on the forehead. This "melon" is actually a sound lens — a sophisticated structure designed to focus the emitted sound waves into a beam which the dolphin can direct where it likes. This sound lens depends on the fact that different lipids (fatty compounds) bend the ultrasonic sound waves traveling through them in different ways. The different lipids have to be arranged in the right shape and sequence in order to focus the returning sound echoes. Each separate lipid is unique and different from normal blubber lipids, and is made by a complicated chemical process, requiring a number of different enzymes.[2]

1. R. Howlett, "Flipper's Secret," *New Scientist,* 154(2088):34–39, June 28, 1997.

2. U. Varanasi, H.R. Feldman, and D.C. Malins, "Molecular Basis for Formation of Lipid Sound Lens in Echolocating Cetaceans," *Nature,* 255(5506):340–343, May 22, 1975.

For such an organ to have evolved, random mutations must have formed the right enzymes to make the
right lipids, and other mutations must have caused the
lipids to be deposited in the right place and shape. A
gradual step-by-step evolution of the organ is not fea-
sible, because until the lipids were fully formed and at
least partly in the right place and shape, they would have
been of no use. Therefore, natural selection would not
have favored incomplete intermediate forms.

MISSING LINKS

Evolutionists believe that whales evolved from
some form of land mammal. According to *Teaching
about Evolution*, page 18, they "evolved from a primitive group of hoofed mammals called *Mesonychids*."

However, there are many changes required for a
whale to evolve from a land mammal. One of them is to
get rid of its pelvis. This would tend to crush the reproductive orifice with propulsive tail movements. But a
shrinking pelvis would not be able to support the hind-
limbs needed for walking. So the hypothetical transitional form would be unsuited to both land and sea, and
hence be extremely vulnerable. Also, the hind part of
the body must twist on the fore part, so the tail's side-
ways movement can be converted to a vertical movement. Seals and dugongs are not anatomically intermediate between land mammals and whales. They have
particular specializations of their own.

The lack of transitional forms in the fossil record
was realized by evolutionary whale experts like the late
E.J. Slijper: "We do not possess a single fossil of the
transitional forms between the aforementioned land
animals [i.e., carnivores and ungulates] and the whales."[3]

The lowest whale fossils in the fossil record show

---

3. E.J. Slijper, *Dolphins and Whales* (Ann Arbor, MI: University of Michigan Press, 1962), p. 17.

they were completely aquatic from the first time they appeared. However, *Teaching about Evolution* is intended as a polemic for evolution. So it reconstructs some recent fossil discoveries to support the whale evolution stories that Slijper believed on faith. On page 18 there is a nice picture of an alleged transitional series between land mammals and whales (drawn at roughly the same size without telling readers that some of the creatures were hugely different in size — see the section about *Basilosaurus* in this chapter). This appears to be derived from an article in *Discover* magazine.[4] The *Discover* list (below) is identical to the *Teaching about Evolution* series except that the latter has *Basilosaurus* as the fourth creature and the *Discover* list has "dates":

- *Mesonychid* (55 million years ago)
- *Ambulocetus* (50 million years ago)
- *Rodhocetus* (46 million years ago)
- *Prozeuglodon* (40 million years ago)

One thing to note is the lack of time for the vast number of changes to occur by mutation and selection. If a mutation results in a new gene, for this new gene to replace the old gene in a population, the individuals carrying the old gene must be eliminated, and this takes time. Population genetics calculations suggest that in 5 million years (one million years longer than the alleged time between *Ambulocetus* and *Rodhocetus*), animals with generation lines of about ten years (typical of whales) could substitute no more than about 1,700 mutations.[5] This is not nearly enough to generate the new information that whales need for aquatic life, even assuming that

---

4. C. Zimmer, "Back to the Sea," *Discover,* January 1995, p. 83.

5. This is explained fully in W.J. ReMine, *The Biotic Message* (St. Paul, MN: St. Paul Science, 1993), chapter 8.

all the hypothetical information-adding mutations required for this could somehow arise. (And as shown in chapter 9, real science shows that this cannot occur.)

AMBULOCETUS

The second in this "transitional series" is the 7-foot (2 m) long *Ambulocetus natans* ("walking whale that swims"). Like the secular media and more "popular" science journals, *Teaching about Evolution* often presents nice neat stories to readers, not the ins and outs of the research methodology, including its limitations. The nice pictures of *Ambulocetus natans* in these publications are based on artists' imaginations, and should be compared with the actual bones found! The difference is illustrated well in the article "A Whale of a Tale?"[6] This article shows that the critical skeletal elements necessary to establish the transition from non-swimming land mammal to whale are (conveniently) missing (see diagram on next page). Therefore, grand claims about the significance of the fossils cannot be critically evaluated. The evolutionary biologist Annalisa Berta commented on the *Ambulocetus* fossil:

> Since the pelvic girdle is not preserved, there is no direct evidence in *Ambulocetus* for a connection between the hind limbs and the axial skeleton. This hinders interpretations of locomotion in this animal, since many of the

6. D. Batten, "A Whale of a Tale?" *Creation Ex Nihilo Technical Journal,* 8(1):2–3, 1994.

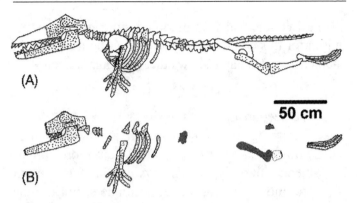

50 cm

(A) Reconstruction of Ambulocetus, *"at the end of the power stroke during swimming."*[7] *The stippled bones were all that were found, and the shaded ones were found 5 m above the rest. (B) With the "additions" removed there really isn't much left of* Ambulocetus*!*

muscles that support and move the hindlimb originate on the pelvis.[7]

Finally, it is dated more recently (by evolutionary dating methods) than undisputed whales, so is unlikely to be a walking ancestor of whales.

BASILOSAURUS

Basilosaurus isis (a.k.a. *euglodon*) is the fourth and last postulated transitional form on page 18 of *Teaching about Evolution*. *Basilosaurus* is Greek for "king lizard," but it was actually a serpent-like sea mammal about 70 feet (21 m) long, with a 5-foot (1.5 m) long skull. It was *10 times* as long as *Ambulocetus*, although the *Teaching about Evolution* book draws them at the

7. J.G.M. Thewissen , S.T. Hussain, and M. Arif, "Fossil Evidence for the Origin of Aquatic Locomotion in Archeocete Whales," *Science,* 263(5144):210–212, January 14, 1994. Perspective by A. Berta, "What is a Whale?," same issue, p. 180–181.

same size — it helps give the desired (false) impression that there is a genuine transitional series.

However, *Basilosaurus* was fully aquatic, so hardly transitional between land mammals and whales. Also, Barbara Stahl, a vertebrate paleontologist and evolutionist, points out:

> The serpentine form of the body and the peculiar shape of the cheek teeth make it plain that these archaeocetes [like *Basilosaurus*] *could not possibly have been the ancestor of modern whales.*

Both modern branches of whales, the toothed whales (Odontoceti) and baleen whales (Mysticeti), appear abruptly in the fossil record. Stahl points out the following regarding the skull structure in both types:

> . . . shows a strange modification *not present, even in a rudimentary way,* in *Basilosaurus* and its relatives: in conjunction with the backward migration of the nostrils on the dorsal surface of the head, the nasal bones have been reduced and carried upwards and the premaxillary and maxillary elements have expanded to the rear to cover the original braincase roof.[8]

Basilosaurus did have small hind limbs (certainly too small for walking), and *Teaching Evolution* says "they were thought to be non-functional." But they were probably used for grasping during copulation, according to even other evolutionists. For example, the evolutionary whale expert Philip Gingerich said, "It seems to

---

8. B.J. Stahl, *Vertebrate History: Problems in Evolution* (New York: McGraw-Hill, 1974), p. 489; emphasis added.

me that they could only have been some kind of sexual and reproductive clasper."[9]

PAKICETUS

Pakicetus inachus is yet another candidate as an intermediate between whales and land mammals in the eyes of some evolutionists. According to evolutionary "dating" methods it is 52 million years old. Since some educational publications have also claimed *Pakicetus* is transitional (see diagram on next page), it is worth discussing although it is absent from *Teaching about Evolution.* This indicates that its authors don't believe *Pakicetus* is a good example of an intermediate. This could be because *Pakicetus* is known only from some cheek teeth and fragments of the skull and lower jaw, so we have no way of knowing whether its locomotion was transitional. The diagram shows the imaginative *reconstruction* taught to schoolteachers and on the cover of *Science,* compared to the *reality* as reported in the same issue. Note that only the *stippled parts* of the skull represent *actual fossil evidence*, while the rest is "reconstructed." But we do know that its hearing mechanism was that of a land mammal and that it was found in fluvial sediments with other land animals.[10] So the evidence shows that it was probably a land mammal, not a transitional form.[11]

G.A. Mchedlidze, a Russian expert on whales, has expressed serious doubts as to whether creatures like *Pakicetus* and *Ambulocetus*, and others — even if accepted as aquatic mammals — can properly be consid-

9. *The Press Enterprise,* July 1, 1990. A–15.

10. P.D. Gingerich, N.A. Wells, D.E. Russell, and S.M.I. Shah, *Science,* 220(4595):403–6, April 22, 1983.

11. A detailed analysis of alleged whale intermediates is A.L. Camp, "The Overselling of Whale Evolution," *Creation Matters*, May–June 1998; online at <http://home.sprynet.com/sprynet/trueorigin/whales.htm>.

Whale 'evolution'?

Pakicetus reconstruction [12]   **What was found** [13]

ered ancestors of modern whales. He sees them instead as a completely isolated group.[14]

VESTIGIAL LEGS?

Many evolutionists support whale evolution by alleging that there are vestigial hind legs buried in their flesh. However, these so-called "remnants" are not useless at all, but help strengthen the reproductive organs — the bones are different in males and females. So they are best explained by creation, not evolution.[15] As with the allegedly functionless limbs of *Basilosaurus*, we should not assume that ignorance of a function means there is no function.

One myth promulgated by some evolutionists says that some whales have been found with hind legs, complete with thigh and knee muscles. However, this story probably grew by legendary accretion from a true account

12. Gingerich, *J. Geol. Educ.*, 31:140–144, 1983.

13. Gingerich et al., *Science*, 220:403–406, 1983.

14. G. A. Mchedlidze, *General Features of the Paleobiological Evolution of Cetacea*, translated from Russian (Rotterdam: A.A. Balkema, 1986), p. 91.

15. J. Bergman and G. Howe, *"Vestigial Organs" Are Fully Functional*, Creation Research Society Monograph No. 4.

of a real sperm whale with a 5.5 inch (14 cm) bump with a 5-inch (12 cm) piece of bone inside. Sperm whales are typically about 62 feet (19 m) long, so this abnormal piece of bone is minute in comparison with the whale — this hardly qualifies as a "leg!"[16]

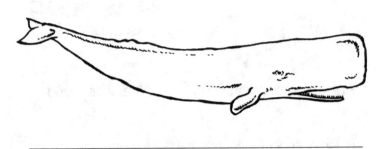

16. C. Wieland, "The Strange Tale of a Leg on a Whale," *Creation,* 20(3):10–13, June–August 1998.

CHAPTER 6

HUMANS:
IMAGES OF GOD OR
ADVANCED APES?

H umans are very different from animals, especially in the ability to use language and logic. *Teaching about Evolution and the Nature of Science* points out a number of contrasts between humans and apes on page 83. But *Teaching about Evolution* forcefully indoctrinates readers with the idea that humans have descended from a simple cell via ape-like ancestors.[1] The arguments used involve alleged "ape-men" and DNA similarities. This chapter analyzes the fossil record, and also discusses the large difference

---

1. *Teaching about Evolution* goes to great pains to "investigate the misconception that humans evolved from apes," pointing out that evolutionists believe that humans and apes share a common ancestor (p. 57, 62, 83). However, a leading atheistic evolutionary paleontologist, the late G.G. Simpson, called this sort of pedantry "pussyfooting." He wrote: "In fact, that earlier ancestor would certainly be called an ape or monkey in popular speech by anyone who saw it. Since the terms ape and monkey are defined by popular usage, man's ancestors were apes or monkeys (or successively both). It is pusillanimous [mean-spirited] if not dishonest for an informed investigator to say otherwise." "The World into Which Darwin Led Us," *Science,* 131:966-969; cited in W.R. Bird, *The Origin of Species: Revisited*, Vol. 1, (Nashville, TN: Thomas Nelson, 1991), p. 233.

in genetic information content between apes and humans.

FOSSIL "APE-MEN"

The best-known fossil "ape men" are the extinct australopithecines (the name means "southern ape"). *Teaching about Evolution* on page 20 illustrates a series of five skulls: *Australopithecus afarensis* ("Lucy"), *A. africanus*, early *Homo*, *H. erectus,* and *H. sapiens* (modern man). However, many evolutionists disagree with this picture. For example, Donald Johanson, the discoverer of "Lucy," places *A. africanus* on a side-branch not leading to man.[2] Anatomist Charles Oxnard performed a detailed analysis of different bones of *A. africanus* and concluded that it did not walk upright in the human manner and was more distinct from both humans and chimpanzees than these are from each other.[3] More recently, Oxnard made the following comments about the australopithecines, including "Lucy:"

It is now recognized widely that the australopithecines are not structurally closely similar to humans, that they must have been living at least in part in arboreal [tree] environments, and that many of the later specimens were contemporaneous [living at the same time] or almost so with the earlier members of the genus *Homo*.[4]

Oxnard, an evolutionist, is one of several experts who do not believe that any of the australopithecines were on the human line.

2. D. Johanson and T.D. White, *Science,* 203:321, 1979; 207:1104, 1980.

3. C.E. Oxnard, *Nature*, 258:389–395, 1975.

4. C.E. Oxnard, *The Order of Man* (New Haven, CT: Yale University Press, 1984).

HUMANS HAVE ALWAYS BEEN HUMANS

Marvin Lubenow, in his book *Bones of Contention*, also shows that the various alleged "ape-men" do not form a smooth sequence in evolutionary "ages," but overlap considerably. He also points out that the various finds are either varieties of true humans (e.g. Neandertals, *Homo erectus*) or non-humans like the australopithecines, which probably includes the so-called *Homo habilis*. There are several lines of evidence to support this:

- Mitochondrial[5] DNA analysis of a Neandertal skeleton found that the sequence differed from modern humans in 22 to 36 places, while the differences among modern humans are from 1 to 24 places.[6] Despite some statistically invalid claims that this makes the Neandertals a separate species, the differences are within the range of modern humans.[7] Also, DNA is quickly broken down by water and oxygen, so under favorable conditions, DNA might last tens of thousands of years at the most.[8] This raises serious

5. Mitochondria (singular mitochondrion) are the structures within cells that help produce energy. They have their own genes which are passed down the female line with the occasional mutation.

6. A group led by Svante Pääbo analyzed one 379-unit sequence (*cf.* a total of 16,500 base pairs in intact human mitochondrial DNA) from an upper arm bone from a Neandertal skeleton supposedly 30,000–100,000 years old. M. Krings, A. Stone, R.W. Schmitz, H. Krainitzki, M Stoneking, and S. Pääbo, "Neandertal DNA Sequences and the Origin of Modern Humans," *Cell,* 90:19–30, 1997.

7. M. Lubenow, "Recovery of Neandertal mtDNA: An Evaluation," *Creation Ex Nihilo Technical Journal,* 12(1):87–97, 1998.

8. T. Lindahl, "Instability and Decay of the Primary Structure of DNA," *Nature,* 362(6422):709–715, 1993. Pääbo himself has found that DNA fragments decay a few hours after death into chains 100-200 units long, that water alone would completely break it down by 50,000 years, and that background radiation would eventually erase DNA information even without water and oxygen, "Ancient DNA," *Scientific American,* 269(5):60–66, 1993.

questions about the 100,000-year "age" that
some scientists have assigned to this skeleton.

- X-ray analysis of the semicircular canals of a
number of "ape-men" skulls showed that the
Homo erectus canals were like those of modern humans, meaning they walked upright. But
those of the *A. africanus* and *A. robustus* were
like those of great apes. This shows they did
not walk upright like humans, but were probably mainly tree-dwelling.[9] "*Homo habilis*"
turned out to be even less "bi-pedal" than the
australopithecines.

HUMAN AND APE SIMILARITIES?

Teaching about Evolution emphasizes physical and
especially DNA similarities between human and other
living organisms, and this is alleged to be evidence for
evolution. However, again this is not a direct finding,
but an *interpretation* of the data.

A *common designer* is another interpretation that
makes sense of the *same* data. An architect commonly
uses the same building material for different buildings,
and a carmaker commonly uses the same parts in different cars. So we shouldn't be surprised if a Designer
for life used the same biochemistry and structures in
many different creatures. Conversely, if all living organisms were totally different, this might look like there
were many designers instead of one.

Another good thing about the common biochemistry is that we can gain nourishment from other living things. Our digestive systems can break down
food into its building blocks, which are then used

9. F. Spoor, B. Wood, and F. Zonneveld, "Implications of Early Hominid
Morphology for Evolution of Human Bipedal Locomotion," *Nature*,
369(6482):645–648, 1994.

either as fuel or for our own building blocks.

Since DNA contains the coding for structures and biochemical molecules, we should expect the most similar creatures to have the most similar DNA. Apes and humans are both mammals, with similar shapes, so have similar DNA. We should expect humans to have more DNA similarities with another mammal like a pig than with a reptile like a rattlesnake. And this is so. Humans are very different from yeast but they have some biochemistry in common, so we should expect human and yeast DNA to be only slightly similar.

So the general pattern of similarities need not be explained by common-ancestry evolution. Furthermore, there are some puzzling anomalies for an evolutionary explanation — similarities between organisms that evolutionists don't believe are closely related. For example, hemoglobin, the complex molecule that carries oxygen in blood and results in its red color, is found in vertebrates. But it is also found in *some* earthworms, starfish, crustaceans, mollusks, and even in some bacteria. Human lysozyme is closer to chicken lysozyme than to that of any other mammal. The a-hemoglobin of crocodiles has more in common with that of chickens (17.5 percent) than that of vipers (5.6 percent), their fellow reptiles.[10] An antigen receptor protein has the same unusual single chain structure in camels and nurse sharks, but this cannot be explained by a common ancestor of sharks and camels.[11]

Similarities between human and ape DNA are often exaggerated. This figure was not derived from a direct comparison of the sequences. Rather, the original

10. H.M. Morris and G.E. Parker, *What is Creation Science?* (Green Forest, AR: Master Books, 1987), p. 52–61. See also M. Denton, *Evolution: A Theory in Crisis*, (Chevy Chase, MD: Adler and Adler, 1986), chapters 7, 12.

11. *Proceedings of the National Academy of Sciences,* 95:11, 804; cited in *New Scientist,* 160(2154):23, October 3, 1998.

paper[12] inferred 97 percent similarity between human and chimp DNA from a rather crude technique called DNA hybridization. In this technique, single strands of human DNA were combined with DNA from chimpanzees and other apes. However, there are other things beside similarity that affect the degree of hybridization.

Actually, even if we grant that degree of hybridization entirely correlates with similarity, there are flaws. When proper statistics are applied to the data,[13] they show that humans and chimps have only about 96 percent similarity. But we frequently hear larger figures bandied about — the alleged similarity grows in the telling!

A point often overlooked is the vast *differences* between different kinds of creatures. Every creature has an encyclopedic information content, so even a small percentage difference means that a lot of information would be required to turn one kind into another. Since humans have an amount of information equivalent to a thousand 500-page books, a 4 percent difference amounts to 40 large books (again, even if we assume that the hybridization data really correlates to gene sequence similarity).

That is, random mutation plus natural selection is expected to generate the information equivalent of 12 million words arranged in a meaningful sequence. This is an impossibility even if we grant the 10 million years asserted by evolutionists. Population genetics calculations show that animals with human-like generation times of about 20 years could substitute no more than about 1,700 mutations in that time.[14]

---

12. C.G. Sibley and J.E. Ahlquist, "DNA Hybridization Evidence of Hominoid Phylogeny: Results from an Expanded Data Set," *Journal of Molecular Evolution,* 26:99–121, 1987.

13. D. Batten, "Human/Chimp DNA Similarity: Evidence for Evolutionary Relationship?" *Creation,* 19(1):21–22, December 1996–February 1997. This article has much important information about this matter.

14. Discussed briefly in chapter 5; for full details, see W.J. ReMine, *The Biotic Message* (St. Paul, MN: St. Paul Science, 1993), chapter 8.

EMBRYO SIMILARITIES?

Teaching about Evolution states on page 1:

As organisms grow from fertilized egg cells into embryos, they pass through many similar developmental stages.

Teaching about Evolution has no embryo drawings. However, many evolutionary books have drawings purportedly showing that embryos look very similar. They are based on the 1874 embryo diagrams by Ernst Haeckel, Darwin's advocate in Germany, whose evolutionary ideas were instrumental in the later rise of Nazism. However, in 1997, a detailed study by Mike Richardson and his team,[15] including actual photographs of a large number of different embryos, showed that embryos of different kinds are *very distinct* (see illustration on next page).

Thus, the only way for Haeckel to have drawn them looking so similar was to have *cheated*. This study was widely publicized in science journals[16] and the secular media, so a book published in 1998 has no excuse for being unaware that the idea of extensive embryonic similarities is outdated and based on fraud.[17]

---

15. M.K. Richardson et al., "There Is No Highly Conserved Embryonic Stage in the Vertebrates: Implications for Current Theories of Evolution and Development," *Anatomy and Embryology,* 196(2):91–106, 1997.

16. E. Pennisi, "Haeckel's Embryos: Fraud Rediscovered," *Science,* 277(5331):1435, September 5, 1997; "Embryonic Fraud Lives On," *New Scientist,* 155(2098):23, September 6, 1997.

17. There is a related idea called embryonic recapitulation, or "ontogeny recapitulates phylogeny," that embryos allegedly pass through stages representing their evolutionary ancestry. This was thoroughly discredited decades ago, and no informed evolutionist uses this "evidence." In particular, no "gill slits" ever form in mammalian embryos; rather, structures called pharyngeal (throat) arches form, and they have no relation to breathing. This idea was based on other fraudulent embryo diagrams by Haeckel.

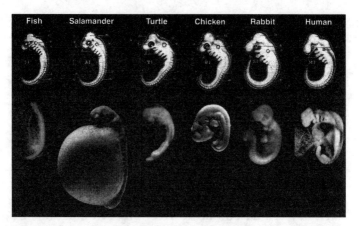

Above, top row: Haeckel's drawings of several different embryos, showing incredible similarity at their early "tailbud" stage.
Bottom row: Richardson's photographs of how the embryos of these same animals really look at the same stage.[18]
From left: Salmo salar, Cryptobranchus allegheniensis, Emys orbicularis, Gallus gallus, Oryctolagus cuniculus, Homo sapiens.

More recently, Richardson and his team confirmed in a letter to *Science* that they still believe in evolution, and that the marked dissimilarities are consistent with this.[19] But this contradicts the usual textbook[20] prediction from Darwinism that embryo development should go through similar stages as Haeckel's faked drawings

---

18. These embryo photos used in this article were kindly supplied by Dr. Michael K. Richardson. They originally appeared in M.K. Richardson et al., footnote 15, © Springer-Verlag GmbH & Co., Tiergartenstrasse, 69121 Heidelberg, Germany. Reproduced here with permission.

19. M.K. Richardson et al., "Haeckel, Embryos, and Evolution," letter to *Science*, 280(5366):983–986, May 15, 1998.

20. B. Alberts et al., *Molecular Biology of the Cell*, (New York: Garland, 1994), p. 32–33.

illustrate. If evolutionary theory predicts both similarities and differences, then it doesn't really predict anything! On the basis of Richardson's letter, evolutionists have claimed he really believes that Haeckel was "basically right."[21] But Richardson confirmed in a later letter to *Science*:

> The core scientific issue remains unchanged: Haeckel's drawings of 1874 are substantially fabricated. In support of this view, I note that his oldest "fish" image is made up of bits and pieces from different animals — some of them mythical. It is not unreasonable to characterize this as "faking." . . . Sadly, it is the discredited 1874 drawings that are used in so many British and American biology textbooks today."[22]

A good account of Haeckel's embryonic fraud was published in *Creation* magazine.[23]

MITOCHONDRIAL EVE

Teaching about Evolution says on page 19:

> According to recent evidence — based on the sequencing of DNA in a part of human cells known as mitochondria — it has been proposed that a small population of modern humans evolved in Africa about 150,000 years

---

21. E.g., the pretentiously named National Center for Science Education, the leading U.S. organization devoted entirely to evolution-pushing — *NCSE Reports*, 17(6):14, officially dated Nov/Dec 1997.

22. M.K. Richardson, "Haeckel's Embryos, Continued," letter to *Science*, 281(5381):1289, August 28, 1998.

23. R. Grigg, "Fraud Rediscovered," *Creation*, 20(2):49–51, 1998; see also R. Grigg, "Ernst Haeckel: Evangelist for Evolution and Apostle of Deceit," *Creation*, 18(2):33–36, 1996, which documents other known frauds by Haeckel.

ago and spread throughout the world, replacing archaic populations of *Homo Sapiens*.

This evidence deals with comparing the DNA from mitochondria. This DNA is inherited only through the mother's line. The similarities indicate that all people on earth are descended from a single human female. Even evolutionists have called her "Mitochondrial Eve."

While this is consistent with the biblical account, we should note that it is not proof. Evolutionists contend that "Mitochondrial Eve" was one of a number of women living. The mitochondrial line of the others would have died out if there were only males in any generation of descendants.

Evolutionists believed they had clear proof against the biblical account, because "Mitochondrial Eve" supposedly lived 200,000 years ago. However, recent evidence shows that mitochondrial DNA mutates far faster than previously thought.[24] If this new evidence is applied to "Mitochondrial Eve," it indicates that she would have lived only 6,000–6,500 years ago.[25] Of course, this is perfectly consistent with the biblically indicated age of the "mother of all living" (Gen. 3:20),[26] but an enigma for evolution/long age beliefs.

Interestingly, there is a parallel account with males: evidence from the Y-chromosome is consistent with all people being descended from a single man.[27] The data

24. T.J. Parsons et al., "A High Observed Substitution Rate in the Human Mitochondrial DNA Control Region," *Nature Genetics,* 15:363–368, 1997.

25. L. Loewe and S. Scherer, "Mitochondrial Eve: The Plot Thickens," *Trends in Ecology and Evolution*, 12(11):422–423, 1997; A. Gibbons, "Calibrating the Mitochondrial Clock," *Science,* 279(5347):28–29, 1998.

26. C. Wieland, "A Shrinking Date for 'Eve,'" *CEN Technical Journal,* 12(1):1–3, 1998.

27. R.L. Dorit, Hiroshi Akashi, and W. Gilbert, "Absence of Polymorphism at the ZFY Locus on the Human Y-Chromosome," *Science,* 268(5214):1183–85, May 26, 1995; perspective in the same issue by S. Pääbo, "The Y-Chromosome and the Origin of All of Us (Men)," p. 1141–1142.

is also consistent with a recent date for this "Y-chromosome Adam."[28]

CONCLUSION

Teaching about Evolution aims to indoctrinate students with the belief that they are evolved animals and ultimately are, in effect, nothing more than a chance rearrangement of matter. A senior writer for *Scientific American* had this inspiring comment:

> Yes, we are all animals, descendants of a vast lineage of replicators sprung from primordial pond scum.[29]

What this leads to is aptly shown by this dialog between two evolutionists. Lanier is a computer scientist; Dawkins is a professor at Oxford and an ardent Darwinist and atheist:

> *Jaron Lanier:* "There's a large group of people who simply are uncomfortable with accepting evolution because it leads to what they perceive as a moral vacuum, in which their best impulses have no basis in nature."

> *Richard Dawkins:* "All I can say is, That's just tough. We have to face up to the truth."[30]

28. D.J. Batten, "Y-Chromosome Adam?" *CEN Technical Journal,* 9(2):139–140, 1995.

29. J. Horgan, "The New Social Darwinists," *Scientific American,* 273(4):150–157, October 1995; quote on p. 151.

30. "Evolution: The Dissent of Darwin," *Psychology Today*, January/February 1997, p. 62.

CHAPTER 7

ASTRONOMY

It may be surprising to see a lot of material about astronomy in a book about evolution. But evolution is not just about ape-like creatures turning into humans. Evolution is a philosophy trying to explain everything without God. Thus, it must be applied to the origin of the universe and solar system. Thus, *Teaching about Evolution and the Nature of Science* presents the prevailing evolutionary view on astronomical origins. Also, *Teaching about Evolution* hopes to diffuse opposition to evolution by a misleading comparison to opposition to heliocentrism (a sun-centered solar system). This chapter critically analyzes typical evolutionary ideas about the universe and solar system, as well as the Galileo controversy.

THE "BIG BANG" THEORY

Teaching about Evolution, page 52, states:

> The origin of the universe remains one of the greatest questions in science. The "big bang" theory places the origin between 10 and 20 billion years ago, when the universe began in a hot dense state; according to this

theory, the universe has been expanding ever since.

Early in the history of the universe, matter, primarily the light atoms hydrogen and helium, clumped together by gravitational attraction to form countless trillions of stars. Billions of galaxies, each of which is a gravitationally bound cluster of billions of stars, now form most of the visible mass in the universe.

Stars produce energy from nuclear reactions, primarily the fusion of hydrogen to form helium. These and other processes have led to the formation of the other elements.

We should first note that even under their perspective, the authors admit that the universe had a beginning. When combined with the *principle of causality*, "everything which has a beginning has a cause," it logically entails that the universe has a cause.[1]

Many Christians support the "big bang" theory because it implies a beginning of the universe. However, other Christians, based on the teaching of the Bible, reject the "big bang."

The "big bang" teaches that the sun and many other stars formed before the earth, while Genesis teaches that they were made on the fourth day *after* the earth, and only about 6,000 years ago rather than 10–20 billion years ago. The "big bang" also entails millions of years of death, disease, and pain before Adam's sin, which contradicts the clear teaching of Scripture, which is thus unacceptable to biblical Christians. Also, the "big bang" theory has many scientific problems as outlined in the

---

1. J.D. Sarfati, "If God Created the Universe, Then Who Created God?" *CEN Technical Journal*, 12(1)20–22, 1998.

next section, and quite a few secular astronomers reject it.

SCIENTIFIC PROBLEMS

Although the above quote from *Teaching about Evolution* rather simplistically moves from the "big bang" to the formation of galaxies and stars, it is not so simple. Dr. James Trefil, professor of physics at George Mason University, Virginia, accepts the "big bang" model, but he admits that there are fundamental problems:

> There shouldn't be galaxies out there at all, and even if there are galaxies, they shouldn't be grouped together the way they are.

He later continues:

> The problem of explaining the existence of galaxies has proved to be one of the thorniest in cosmology. By all rights, they just shouldn't be there, yet there they sit. It's hard to convey the depth of the frustration that this simple fact induces among scientists.[2]

The creationist cosmologist, Dr. John Rankin, also showed mathematically in his Ph.D. thesis that galaxies would not form from the "big bang."[3]

The formation of stars after the alleged "big bang" is also a huge problem. The creationist astronomer, Dr. Danny Faulkner, pointed out:

2. J. Trefil, *The Dark Side of the Universe* (New York: Macmillan Publishing Company, 1988), p. 3 and 55; see also W. Gitt, "What about the 'Big Bang?' " *Creation,* 20(3):42–44, June–August 1998.

3. J. Rankin, *Protogalaxy Formation from Inhomogeneities in Cosmological Models*, Ph.D. thesis, Adelaide University, May/June 1977.

Stars supposedly condensed out of vast clouds of gas, and it has long been recognized that the clouds don't spontaneously collapse and form stars, they need to be pushed somehow to be started. There have been a number of suggestions to get the process started, and almost all of them require having stars to start with [e.g. a shockwave from an exploding star causing compression of a nearby gas cloud]. This is the old chicken and egg problem; it can't account for the origin of stars in the first place.[4]

Another problem is cooling a gas cloud enough for it to collapse. This requires molecules to radiate the heat away. But as *Teaching about Evolution* points out in the quote earlier, the "big bang" would produce mainly hydrogen and helium, unsuitable for making the molecules apart from H_2, which would be destroyed rapidly under the ultraviolet light present, and which usually needs dust grains for its formation — and dust grains require heavier elements. The heavier elements, according to the theory, require *pre-existing* stars. Again, there is a chicken and egg problem of needing stars to produce stars.

Abraham Loeb of Harvard's Center for Astrophysics says: "The truth is that we don't understand star formation at a fundamental level."[5]

ASSUMPTIONS

The "big bang" is actually based on a non-scientific *assumption* called the *cosmological principle*,

---

4. " 'He Made the Stars Also' — interview with creationist astronomer Danny Faulkner," *Creation,* 19(4):42–44, September–November 1997.

5. Quoted by Marcus Chown, "Let There Be Light," *New Scientist,* 157(2120):26–30, (7 February 1998). See also "Stars could not have come from the 'big bang,'" sidebar, *Creation,* 20(3):42–43, June–August 1998.

which states that an observer's view of the universe depends neither on the direction in which he looks nor on his location. That is, the earth is nowhere special. However, there are alternatives to the "big bang" that reject this assumption. One has been proposed in the book *Starlight and Time*[6] by Dr. Russell Humphreys, a nuclear physicist working with Sandia National Laboratories in Albuquerque, New Mexico. He has developed a new cosmology which uses the same theoretical foundation as all modern cosmologies including the "big-bang" — Einstein's theory of general relativity.

This results in a cosmology which allows for the formation of the universe in the biblical time-frame, as well as the traveling of light to earth from stars billions of light years distant. This plausible solution to a commonly raised skeptical problem works because general relativity shows that time is different in different reference frames with different gravitational fields. So the universe could have been made in six ordinary days in earth's reference frame, but the light had ample time to travel in an extraterrestrial reference frame. However, as with all scientific theories, we should not be too dogmatic about this model, although it seems very good.

THE SOLAR SYSTEM

Teaching about Evolution, page 52, states:

> The sun, the earth and the rest of the solar system formed from a nebular cloud of dust and gas 4.5 billion years ago.

As usual, the book's authors are dogmatic about what happened, although they weren't there. However,

---

6. Russell Humphreys, *Starlight and Time* (Green Forest, AR: Master Books, Inc., 1994).

this *nebular hypothesis* has many problems. One authority summarized: "The clouds are too hot, too magnetic, and they rotate too rapidly."[7]

One major problem can be shown by accomplished skaters spinning on ice. As skaters pull their arms in, they spin faster. This effect is due to what physicists call the *Law of Conservation of Angular Momentum.* Angular momentum = mass x velocity x distance from the center of mass, and always stays constant in an isolated system. When the skaters pull their arms in, the distance from the center decreases, so they spin faster or else angular momentum would not stay constant. In the alleged formation of our sun from a nebula in space, the same effect would have occurred as the gases contracted into the center to form the sun. This would have caused the sun to spin very rapidly. Actually, our sun spins very slowly, while the planets move very rapidly around the sun. In fact, although the sun has over 99 percent of the mass of the solar system, it has only 2 percent of the angular momentum. This pattern is directly opposite to the pattern predicted for the nebular hypothesis. Evolutionists have tried to solve this problem, but a well-known solar system scientist, Dr. Stuart Ross Taylor, has said in a recent book, "The ultimate origin of the solar system's angular momentum remains obscure."[8]

Another problem with the nebular hypothesis is the formation of the gaseous planets. As the gas would pull together into the planets, the young sun would pass through what is called the *T-Tauri phase.* In this phase, the sun would give off an intense solar wind, far more

---

7. S.F. Dermott, editor, *The Origin of the Solar System*, "The Origin of the Solar System," by H. Reeves (New York: John Wiley & Sons, 1978), p. 9.

8. S.R. Taylor, *Solar System Evolution: A New Perspective* (New York: Cambridge University Press, 1992), p. 53.

intense than at present. This solar wind would have driven excess gas and dust out of the still-forming solar system and thus there would no longer be enough of the light gases left to form Jupiter and the other three giant gas planets. This would leave these four gas planets smaller than we find them today.[9]

HELIOCENTRISM

SCIENCE VERSUS RELIGION?

Like much secular literature, *Teaching about Evolution* presents a rather simplistic and even misleading account of the Galileo controversy. It was certainly not a simple case of science versus the Church (p. 27–30).[10] However, *Teaching about Evolution*, to its credit, does not promote the common skeptical canard that the Bible teaches that the earth is flat and that this belief was widespread in medieval times.

Isaiah 40:22 refers to "the circle of the earth," or in the Italian translation, *globo*. The Hebrew is *khug* (gWj) = sphericity or roundness. Even if the translation "circle" is adhered to, think about Neil Armstrong in space — to him, the spherical earth would have appeared circular regardless of which direction he viewed it from.

Also, Jesus Christ's prophecy about His second coming in Luke 17:34–36 implies that He knew about a round earth. He stated that different people on earth would experience night, morning, and midday at the same time. This is possible because the spheroidal earth is rotating on its axis, which allows the sun to shine on different areas at different times. But it would be an inconceivable prophecy if Christ believed in a flat earth.

9. W. Spencer, "Revelations in the Solar System," *Creation,* 19(3):26–29, June–August 1997.

10. R. Grigg, "The Galileo Twist," *Creation,* 19(4):30–32, September–November 1997.

The idea that Columbus had to disprove that the earth was flat is a myth started by Washington Irving in his 1828 book *The Life and Voyages of Christopher Columbus*. This was a self-confessed mixture of fact and fiction. The historian J.B. Russell has documented that nearly all Christian scholars who have ever discussed the earth's shape have assented to its roundness.[11]

As many historians of science have noticed, the first to oppose Galileo was the scientific establishment. The prevailing "scientific" wisdom of his day was the Aristotelian/Ptolemaic theory. This was an unwieldy *geocentric* system; that is, with the earth at the center of the universe and other heavenly bodies in highly complex orbits around the earth. As Arthur Koestler wrote:

> But there existed a powerful body of men whose hostility to Galileo never abated: the Aristotelians at the Universities. . . . Innovation is a twofold threat to academic mediocrities: it endangers their oracular authority, and it evokes the deeper fear that their whole laboriously constructed edifice might collapse. The academic backwoods-men have been the curse of genius . . . it was this threat — not Bishop Dantiscus or Pope Paul III — which had cowed Canon Koppernigk [i.e., Copernicus] into silence. . . .
>
> The first serious attack on religious grounds came also not from clerical quarters,

---

11. Jeffrey Burton Russell, *Inventing the Flat Earth: Columbus & Modern Historians* (Praeger, 1991). Prof. Russell can find only five obscure writers in the first 1500 years of the Christian era who denied that the earth was a globe. But he documents a large number of writers, including Thomas Aquinas, who affirmed the earth's sphericity. See also *Creation Ex Nihilo* 14(4):21, 16(2):48–9.

but from a layman — none other than delle Colombe, the leader of the [ardent Aristotelian] league. . . .

The earthly nature of the moon, the existence of sunspots meant the abandonment of the [pagan!] Aristotelian doctrines on the perfect and unchangeable nature of the celestial spheres.[12]

Conversely, at first the church was open to Galileo's discoveries. Astronomers of the Jesuit Order, "the intellectual spearhead of the Catholic Church," even improved on them. Only 50 years later, they were teaching this theory in China. They also protected Johannes Kepler, who discovered that planets move in ellipses around the sun. Even the Pope, Paul V, received Galileo in friendly audience.

The leading Roman Catholic theologian of the day, Cardinal Robert Bellarmine said it was "excellent good sense" to claim that Galileo's model was mathematically simpler. And he said:

If there were a real proof that the Sun is in the centre of the universe, that the Earth is in the third sphere, and that the Sun does not go round the Earth but the Earth round the Sun, then we should have to proceed with great circumspection in explaining passages of Scripture which appear to teach the contrary, and we should rather have to say that we did not understand them than declare an opinion false which has been proved to be true.

12. A. Koestler, *The Sleepwalkers: A History of Man's Changing Vision of the Universe* (London: Hutchinson, 1959), p. 427.

> But I do not think there is any such proof
> since none has been shown to me.[13]

This shows people were allowed to state that the heliocentric (sun-centered) system was a superior hypothesis to the earth-centered system. Also, the leading theologian was prepared to change his understanding of Scripture, if the system were proven — i.e., to correct his misunderstanding that Scripture taught the Ptolemaic system of astronomy. The misunderstanding arose because people failed to realize that biblical passages must be understood in terms of what the *author was trying to convey*. As shown below, passages referring to the rising and setting sun (for example, Eccles. 1:5) were not intended to teach a particular astronomical model like Ptolemy's. Rather, they are describing events in understandable, but *still scientifically valid* terms that even modern people use, so any reader will understand what is meant.

Another problem was that some of the clergy supported the Ptolemaic system using verses in the Psalms. However, the Psalms are clearly poetic, not historical like Genesis.[14] Thus, they were never intended to be used as a basis for a cosmological model. This can be shown by analyzing the context of Psalm 93:1: "The world is firmly established; it cannot be moved."

We should understand the terms as used by the biblical authors. Let's read the next verse, "[God's] throne *is* established of old," where the same word Hebrew *kown* is translated "established" [i.e., stable, secure, enduring, not necessarily stationary, immobile].

---

13. Ibid., p. 447–448.

14. Principles of biblical interpretation, clearly contrasting the historical Book of Genesis with the poetic Book of Psalms, are discussed in detail in R.M. Grigg, "Should Genesis Be Taken Literally?" *Creation,* 16(1):38–41, December 1993– February 1994; also footnote 11.

Also, the same Hebrew word for "moved" (*mowt*) is used in Psalm 16:8, "I shall not be moved." Surely, even skeptics wouldn't accuse the Bible of teaching that the Psalmist was rooted to one spot! He meant that he would not stray from the path that God had set for him. So the earth "cannot be moved" can also mean that it will not stray from the precise orbital and rotational pattern God has set for it. Life on earth requires that the earth's orbit is at just the right distance from the sun for liquid water to exist. Also, that the earth's rotational axis is at just the right angle from the ecliptic (orbital plane) so that temperature differences are not too extreme.

From a scientific point of view, Bellarmine was right to insist that the burden of proof belonged to the proposers of the new system. Certainly, the heliocentric system was more elegant, which is what appealed to Galileo and Kepler, and the geocentric system was very unwieldy. But this was not the same as proof. In fact, some of Galileo's "proofs" — for example, his theory of the tides — were fallacious.

DID GALILEO DISPROVE THE BIBLE?

Galileo was shocked at the thought — he accepted biblical authority more faithfully than many Christian leaders do today. It's ironic that the four heroes of heliocentrism mentioned by *Teaching about Evolution* — Copernicus, Galileo, Kepler, and Newton — were all young-earth creationists! But, of course, *Teaching about Evolution* does not tell its readers this fact!

Galileo and his opponents would have avoided all trouble by realizing that all motion must be described with respect to a *reference frame*. Think about travelling in a car at 60 mph. What does this mean? It means that you and the car are both moving at 60 mph *relative to the ground*. But relative to the *car*, you are basically not moving — that's why you can read the speedometer, and talk to other passengers. But imagine a head-on crash with another car moving at 60 mph in the opposite direction. As far as you're concerned, it would be as if you were standing still and a car drove into you at 120 mph — which is why head-on collisions are the worst. Crashing into a stationary car isn't nearly as bad. And colliding with a car in front moving at 50 mph would be like colliding with a stationary car if you were traveling at only 10 mph. In physics, one is free to choose the most convenient reference frame, and all are equally valid.

Some skeptics have asserted that biblical passages such as Ecclesiastes 1:5, saying that the sun rises and sets, are errors. But the correct understanding of the Bible's descriptions of motion is determined by the *reference frame* it is using. It should be obvious that the Bible is using the *earth* as a convenient reference frame, as we often do today. So the skeptics' accusations are absurd — modern astronomers also refer to "sunset" and "sunrise," without any suggestion of error. And when drivers see a speed limit sign of 60 mph, they know perfectly well that it means 60 mph *relative to the ground*, not the sun! So the Bible is more scientific than its modern critics. And although even Psalm 93:1, cited above, is not teaching about cosmology, it is actually scientifically accurate — the earth cannot be moved relative to the earth!

CHAPTER 8

HOW OLD IS THE EARTH?

For particles-to-people evolution to have occurred, the earth would need to be billions of years old. So *Teaching about Evolution and the Nature of Science* presents what it claims is evidence for vast time spans. This is graphically illustrated in a chart on pages 36–37: man's existence is in such a tiny segment at the end of a 5-billion-year time-line that it has to be diagrammatically magnified twice to show up.

On the other hand, basing one's ideas on the Bible gives a very different picture. The Bible states that man was made six days after creation, about 6,000 years ago. So a time-line of the world constructed on biblical data would have man almost at the beginning, not the end. If we took the same 15-inch (39 cm) time-line as does *Teaching about Evolution* to represent the biblical history of the Earth, man would be about 1/1000th of a mm away from the beginning! Also, Christians, by definition, take the statements of Jesus Christ seriously. He said: "But from the beginning of the creation God made them male and female" (Mark 10:6), which would make sense with the proposed biblical time-line, but is diametrically opposed to the *Teaching about Evolution* time-line.

This chapter analyzes rock formation and dating methods in terms of what these two competing models would predict.

THE ROCKS

The vast thicknesses of sedimentary rocks around the world are commonly used as evidence for vast age. First, *Teaching about Evolution* gives a useful definition on page 33:

> Sedimentary rocks are formed when solid materials carried by wind and water accumulate in layers and then are compressed by overlying deposits. Sedimentary rocks sometimes contain fossils formed from the parts of organisms deposited along with other solid materials.

The "deep time" indoctrination comes with the statement "often reaching great thicknesses over long periods of time." However, this goes beyond the evidence. Great thicknesses could conceivably be produced either by a little water over long periods, or a lot of water over short periods. We have already discussed how different biases can result in different *interpretations* of the *same* data, in this case the rock layers. It is a *philosophical decision*, not a scientific one, to prefer the former interpretation. Because sedimentation usually occurs slowly today, it is *assumed* that it must have always occurred slowly. If so, then the rock layers must have formed over vast ages. The philosophy that processes have always occurred at roughly constant rates ("the present is the key to the past") is often called *uniformitarianism*.

Uniformitarianism was defined this way in my own university geology class in 1983, and was contrasted with *catastrophism*. But more recently, the word "uniformitarianism" has been applied in other contexts to mean also constancy of natural laws, sometimes called "methodological uniformitarianism," as opposed to what some have called "substantive uniformitarianism."

It should also be pointed out that uniformitarian geologists have long allowed for the occasional (localized) catastrophic event. However, modern historical geology grew out of this general "slow and gradual" principle, which is still the predominantly preferred framework of explanation for any geological formation. Nevertheless, the evidence for catastrophic formation is so pervasive that there is a growing body *of neo-catastrophists*. But because of their naturalistic bias, they prefer, of course, to reject the explanation of the Genesis (global) flood.

However, a cataclysmic globe-covering (and fossil-forming) flood would have eroded huge quantities of sediment, and deposited them elsewhere. Many organisms would have been buried very quickly and fossilized.

Also, recent catastrophes show that violent events like the flood described in Genesis could form many rock layers very quickly. The Mount St. Helens eruption in Washington state produced 25 feet (7.6 meters) of finely layered sediment in a *single afternoon!*[1] And a rapidly pumped sand slurry was observed to deposit 3 to 4 feet (about 1 meter) of fine layers on a beach over

---

1. S.A. Austin, "Mount St. Helens and Catastrophism," *Proceedings of the First International Conference on Creationism*, 1:3–9, ed. R.E. Walsh, R.S. Crowell, Creation Science Fellowship, Pittsburgh, PA, USA, 1986; for a simplified article, see K. Ham, "I Got Excited at Mount St. Helens!" *Creation*, 15(3):14–19, June–August 1993.

an area the size of a football field.[2] Sedimentation experiments by the creationist Guy Berthault, sometimes working with non-creationists, have shown that fine layers can form by a self-sorting mechanism during the settling of differently sized particles.[3]

In one of Berthault's experiments, finely layered sandstone and diatomite rocks were broken into their constituent particles, and allowed to settle under running water at various speeds. It was found that the same layer thicknesses were reproduced, regardless of flow rate. This suggests that the original rock was produced by a similar self-sorting mechanism, followed by cementing of the particles together.[4] The journal *Nature* reported similar experiments by evolutionists a decade after Berthault's first experiments.[5]

So when we start from the bias that the Bible is God's Word and is thus true, we can derive reasonable interpretations of the data. Not that every problem has been solved, but many of them have been.

Conversely, how does the "slow and gradual" explanation fare? Think how long dead organisms normally last. Scavengers and rotting normally remove all traces within weeks. Dead jellyfish normally melt away in days. Yet *Teaching about Evolution* has a photo of a fossil jellyfish on page 36. It clearly couldn't have been buried slowly, but must have been buried quickly by

2. Don Batten, "Sandy Stripes: Do Many Layers Mean Many Years?" *Creation*, 19(1):39–40, December 1996–February 1997.

3. P. Julien, Y. Lan, and G. Berthault, "Experiments on Stratification of Heterogeneous Sand Mixtures," *Creation Ex Nihilo Technical Journal*, 8(1):37–50, 1994.

4. G. Berthault, "Experiments on Lamination of Sediments," *Creation Ex Nihilo Technical Journal*, 3:25–29, 1988.

5. H.A. Makse, S. Havlin, P.R. King, and H.E. Stanley, "Spontaneous Stratification in Granular Mixtures," *Nature*, 386(6623):379–382, March 27, 1997. See also A. Snelling, "*Nature* Finally Catches Up," *CEN Technical Journal*, 11(2):125–6, 1997.

sediments carried by water. This water would also have contained dissolved minerals, which would have caused the sediments to have been cemented together, and so hardened quickly.

The booklet *Stones and Bones*[6] shows other fossils that must have formed rapidly. One is a 7-foot (2m) long ichthyosaur (extinct fish-shaped marine reptile) fossilized while giving birth. Another is a fish fossilized in the middle of its lunch. And there is a vertical tree trunk that penetrates several rock layers (hence the term *polystrate* fossil). If the upper sedimentary layers really took millions or even hundreds of years to form, then the top of the tree trunk would have rotted away.

Ironically, NASA scientists accept that there have been "catastrophic floods" on Mars[7] that carved out canyons[8] although no liquid water is present today. But they deny that a global flood happened on earth, where there is enough water to cover the whole planet to a depth of 1.7 miles (2.7 km) if it were completely uniform, and even now covers 71 percent of the earth's surface! If it weren't for the fact that the Bible teaches it, they probably wouldn't have any problem with a global flood on earth. This demonstrates again how the biases of scientists affect their interpretation of the evidence.

RADIOMETRIC DATING

As shown above, the evidence from the geological record is consistent with catastrophes, and there are many features that are hard to explain by

---

6. Carl Wieland, *Stones and Bones*, (Green Forest, AR: Master Books, Inc., 1994).

7. R.A. Kerr, "Pathfinder Tells a Geologic Tale with One Starring Role," *Science,* 279(5348):175, January 9, 1998.

8. O. Morton, "Flatlands," *New Scientist,* 159(2143):36–39, July 18, 1998.

slow and gradual processes. However, evolutionists point to dating methods that allegedly support deep time. The best known is radiometric dating. This is accurately described on page 35 of *Teaching about Evolution*:

> Some elements, such as uranium, undergo radioactive decay to produce other elements. By measuring the quantities of radioactive elements and the elements into which they decay in rocks, geologists can determine how much time has elapsed since the rock has cooled from an initially molten state.

However, the deep time "determination" is an *interpretation*; the actual scientific data are isotope ratios. Each chemical element usually has several different forms, or isotopes, which have different masses. There are other possible interpretations, depending on the assumptions. This can be illustrated with an hourglass. When it is up-ended, sand flows from the top container to the bottom one at a rate that can be

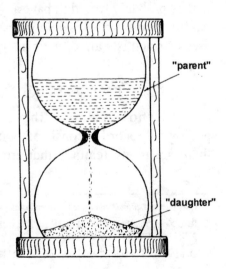

An hourglass "clock" tells us the elapsed time by comparing the amount of sand in the top bowl ("parent") with the amount in the bottom bowl ("daughter").

measured. If we observe an hourglass with the sand still flowing, we can determine how long ago it was up-ended from the quantities of sand in both containers and the flow rate. Or can we? First, we must assume three things:

1. We know the quantities of sand in both containers at the start. Normally, an hourglass is up-ended when the top container is empty. But if this were not so, then it would take less time for the sand to fill the new bottom container to a particular level.

2. The rate has stayed constant. For example, if the sand had become damp recently, it would flow more slowly now than in the past. If the flow were greater in the past, it would take less time for the sand to reach a certain level than it would if the sand had always flowed at the present rate.

3. The system has remained closed. That is, no sand has been added or removed from either container. However, suppose that, without your knowledge, sand had been added to the bottom container, or removed from the top container. Then if you calculated the time since the last up-ending by measuring the sand in both containers, it would be longer than the actual time.

Teaching about Evolution addresses assumption 2:

> For example, it requires that the rate of radioactive decay is constant over time and is not influenced by such factors as temperature and pressure — conclusions supported by extensive research in physics.

It is true that in today's world, radioactive decay rates seem constant, and are unaffected by heat or pressure. However, we have tested decay rates for only about 100 years, so we can't be sure that they were constant over the alleged billions of years. Nuclear physicist Dr. Russell Humphreys suggests that decay rates were faster during creation week, and have remained constant since then. There is some basis for this, for example radiohalo analysis, but it is still tentative.

Teaching about Evolution also addresses assumption 3:

> It also assumes that the rocks being analyzed have not been altered over time by migration of atoms in or out of the rocks, which requires detailed information from both the geologic and chemical sciences.

This is a huge assumption. Potassium and uranium, both common parent elements, are easily dissolved in water, so could be leached out of rocks. Argon, produced by decay from potassium, is a gas, so moves quite readily.

ANOMALIES

There are many examples where the dating methods give "dates" that are wrong for rocks of *known* historical age. One example is rock from a dacite lava dome at Mount St. Helens volcano. Although we know the rock was formed in 1986, the rock was "dated" by the potassium-argon (K-Ar) method as 0.35 ± 0.05 million years old.[9] Another example is K-Ar "dating" of five andesite lava flows from Mt. Ngauruhoe in New

---

9. S.A. Austin, "Excess Argon within Mineral Concentrates from the New Dacite Lava Dome at Mount St. Helens Volcano," *CEN Technical Journal,* 10(3):335–343, 1986.

Zealand. The "dates" ranged from <0.27 to 3.5 million years — but one lava flow occurred in 1949, three in 1954, and one in 1975!

What happened was that excess radiogenic argon ($^{40}Ar^*$) from the magma (molten rock) was retained in the rock when it solidified. The secular scientific literature also lists many examples of excess $^{40}Ar^*$ causing "dates" of millions of years in rocks of known historical age. This excess appears to have come from the upper mantle, below the earth's crust. This is consistent with a young world — the argon has had too little time to escape.[10]

• If excess $^{40}Ar^*$ can cause exaggerated dates for rocks of *known* age, then why should we trust the method for rocks of *unknown* age?

Another problem is the conflicting dates between different methods. If two methods disagree, then at least one of them must be wrong. For example, in Australia, some wood was buried by a basalt lava flow, as can be seen from the charring. The wood was "dated" by radiocarbon (^{14}C) analysis at about 45,000 years old, but the basalt was "dated" by the K-Ar method at c. 45 million years old![11] Other fossil wood from Upper Permian

10. A.A. Snelling, "The Cause of Anomalous Potassium-Argon 'Ages' for Recent Andesite Flows at Mt. Ngauruhoe, New Zealand, and the Implications for Potassium-Argon 'Dating,'" *Proceedings of the Fourth International Conference on Creationism, Creation Science Fellowship, Pittsburgh*, ed. E. Walsh, 1998, p. 503–525.This document lists many examples. For example, six were reported by D. Krummenacher, "Isotopic Composition of Argon in Modern Surface Rocks," *Earth and Planetary Science Letters*, 8:109–117, 1970; five were reported by G.B. Dalrymple, "$^{40}Ar/^{36}Ar$ Analysis of Historic Lava Flows," *Earth and Planetary Science Letters*, 6:47–55, 1969. Also, a large excess was reported in D.E. Fisher, "Excess Rare Gases in a Subaerial Basalt from Nigeria," *Nature*, 232:60–61, 1970.

11. A.A. Snelling, "Radiometric Dating in Conflict," *Creation*, 20(1):24–27, December 1997–February 1998.

rock layers has been found with ^{14}C still present. Detectable ^{14}C would have all disintegrated if the wood were really older than 50,000 years, let alone the 250 million years that evolutionists assign to these Upper Permian rock layers.[12]

According to the Bible's chronology, great age cannot be the true cause of the observed isotope ratios. Anomalies like the above are good supporting evidence, but we are not yet sure of the true cause in all cases. A group of creationist Ph.D. geologists and physicists from Answers in Genesis, the Creation Research Society, and the Institute for Creation Research are currently working on this topic. Their aim is to find out the precise geochemical and/or geophysical causes of the observed isotope ratios.[13] One promising lead is questioning Assumption 1 — the initial conditions are not what the evolutionists think, but are affected, for example, by the chemistry of the rock that melted to form the magma.

EVIDENCE FOR A YOUNG WORLD

Actually, 90 percent of the methods that have been used to estimate the age of the earth point to an age far less than the billions of years asserted by evolutionists. A few of them:

- Red blood cells and hemoglobin have been found in some (unfossilized!) dinosaur bone. But these could not last more than a few thousand years — certainly not the 65 million years from when evolutionists think the last dinosaur lived.[14]

12. A.A. Snelling, "Stumping Old-Age Dogma," *Creation,* 20(4):48–50, September–November 1998.

13. *Acts and Facts,* Institute for Creation Research, 27(7), July 1998.

14. C. Wieland, "Sensational Dinosaur Blood Report!" *Creation,* 19(4):42–43, September–November 1997; based on research by M. Schweitzer and T. Staedter, "The Real Jurassic Park," *Earth,* June 1997, p. 55–57.

- The earth's magnetic field has been decaying so fast that it couldn't be more than about 10,000 years old. Rapid reversals during the flood year and fluctuations shortly after just caused the field energy to drop even faster.[15]

- Helium is pouring into the atmosphere from radioactive decay, but not much is escaping. But the total amount in the atmosphere is only 1/2000th of that expected if the atmosphere were really billions of years old. This helium originally escaped from rocks. This happens quite fast, yet so much helium is still in some rocks that it couldn't have had time to escape — certainly not billions of years.[16]

- A supernova is an explosion of a massive star — the explosion is so bright that it briefly outshines the rest of the galaxy. The supernova remnants (SNRs) should keep expanding for hundreds of thousands of years, according to the physical equations. Yet there are no very old, widely expanded (Stage 3) SNRs, and few moderately old (Stage 2) ones in our galaxy, the Milky Way, or in its satellite galaxies, the Magellanic clouds. This is just what we would expect if these galaxies had not existed long enough for wide expansion.[17]

15. D.R. Humphreys, "Reversals of the Earth's Magnetic Field During the Genesis Flood," *Proceedings of the First International Conference on Creationism,* vol. 2 (Pittsburgh, PA: Creation Science Fellowship, 1986), p. 113–126; J.D. Sarfati, "The Earth's Magnetic Field: Evidence That the Earth Is Young," *Creation,* 20(2):15–19, March–May 1998.

16. L. Vardiman, *The Age of the Earth's Atmosphere: A Study of the Helium Flux through the Atmosphere* (El Cajon, CA: Institute for Creation Research, 1990); J.D. Sarfati, "Blowing Old-Earth Belief Away: Helium Gives Evidence That the Earth Is Young," *Creation,* 20(3):19–21, June–August 1998.

17. K. Davies, "Distribution of Supernova Remnants in the Galaxy," *Proceedings of the Third International Conference on Creationism,* ed. R.E. Walsh, 1994, p. 175–184; J.D. Sarfati, "Exploding Stars Point to a Young Universe," *Creation,* 19(3):46–49, June–August 1998.

- The moon is slowly receding from earth at about 1-1/2 inches (4cm) per year, and the rate would have been greater in the past. But even if the moon had started receding from being in contact with the earth, it would have taken only 1.37 billion years to reach its present distance. This gives a *maximum possible* age of the moon — not the *actual* age. This is far too young for evolution (and much younger than the radiometric "dates" assigned to moon rocks).[18]

- Salt is pouring into the sea much faster than it is escaping. The sea is not nearly salty enough for this to have been happening for billions of years. Even granting generous assumptions to evolutionists, the seas could not be more than 62 million years old — far younger than the billions of years believed by evolutionists. Again, this indicates a *maximum* age, not the *actual* age.[19]

A number of other processes inconsistent with billions of years are given in the *AiG* pamphlet *Evidence for a Young World*, by Dr. Russell Humphreys.

Creationists admit that they can't *prove* the age of the earth using a particular scientific method. They realize that all science is tentative because we do not have all the data, especially when dealing with the past. This is true of both creationist and evolutionist scientific arguments — evolutionists have had to abandon many "proofs" for evolution as well. For example, the

---

18. D. DeYoung, "The Earth-Moon System," *Proceedings of the Second International Conference on Creationism*, vol. 2, ed. R.E. Walsh and C.L Brooks, 1990, 79–84; J.D. Sarfati, "The Moon: The Light That Rules the Night," *Creation*, 20(4):36–39, September–November 1998.

19. S.A. Austin and D.R. Humphreys, "The Sea's Missing Salt: A Dilemma for Evolutionists," *Proceedings of the Second International Conference on Creationism*, Vol. 2, 1990, 17–33; J.D. Sarfati, "Salty Seas: Evidence for a Young Earth," *Creation*, 21(1):16–17, December 1998–February 1999.

atheistic evolutionist W.B. Provine admits: "Most of what I learned of the field in graduate (1964–68) school is either wrong or significantly changed."[20] Creationists understand the limitations of these dating methods better than evolutionists who claim that they can use certain present processes to "prove" that the earth is billions of years old. In reality, all age-dating methods, including those which point to a young earth, rely on unprovable assumptions.

Creationists ultimately date the earth using the chronology of the Bible. This is because they believe that this is an accurate eyewitness account of world history, which can be shown to be consistent with much data.

---

20. *Teaching about Evolution and the Nature of Science,* A Review by Dr. Will B. Provine, cited on February 18, 1999. Available online from http://fp.bio.utk.edu/darwin/NAS_guidebook/provine_1.html.

Addendum: John Woodmorappe has just published a detailed study demonstrating the fallacy of radiometric "dating," including the "high-tech" isochron method: *The Mythology of Modern Dating Methods* (El Cajon, CA: Institute for Creation Research, 1999).

CHAPTER 9

IS THE DESIGN EXPLANATION LEGITIMATE?

As pointed out in previous chapters, *Teaching about Evolution* frequently dismisses creation as "unscientific" and "religious." Creationists frequently point out that creation occurred in the past, so cannot be directly observed by experimental science — and that the same is true of large-scale evolution. But evolution or creation might conceivably have left some *effects* that can be observed. This chapter discusses the criteria that are used in everyday life to determine whether something has been designed, and applies them to the living world. The final section discusses whether design is a legitimate explanation for life's complexity or whether naturalistic causes should be invoked *a priori*.

HOW DO WE DETECT DESIGN?

People detect intelligent design all the time. For example, if we find arrowheads on a desert island, we can assume they were made by someone, *even if we cannot see the designer.*[1]

There is an obvious difference between writing by an intelligent person, e.g. Shakespeare's plays, and a random letter sequence like WDLMNLTDTJBKWIRZ REZLMQCOP.[2] There is also an obvious difference between Shakespeare and a repetitive sequence like ABCDABCDABCD. The latter is an example of *order*, which must be distinguished from Shakespeare, which is an example of *specified complexity*.

We can also tell the difference between messages written in sand and the results of wave and wind action. The carved heads of the U.S. presidents on Mt. Rushmore are clearly different from erosional features. Again, this is specified complexity. Erosion produces either irregular shapes or highly ordered shapes like sand dunes, but not presidents' heads or writing.

Another example is the SETI program (Search for Extraterrestrial Intelligence). This would be pointless if there was no way of determining whether a certain type of signal from outer space would be proof of an intelligent sender. The criterion is, again, a signal with a high level of specified complexity — this would prove that there was an intelligent sender, *even if we had no other idea of the sender's nature.* But neither a random nor a repetitive sequence would be proof. Natural processes produce radio noise from outer space, while pulsars produce regular signals. Actually, pulsars were first mistaken for signals by people eager to believe in extraterrestrials, but this is because they mistook order

---

1. Ken Ham, "How Would You Answer . . . ?" *Creation Ex Nihilo*, 20(3):32–34, June–August 1998. An expanded version is available in his booklet *Is there Really a God?* (Answers in Genesis, 1998).

2. Example of a random sequence from the atheistic evolutionary propagandist R. Dawkins, *The Blind Watchmaker: Why the Evidence of Evolution Reveals a Universe without Design* (New York: W.W. Norton, 1986), p. 47.

for complexity. So evolutionists (as are nearly all SETI proponents) are prepared to use high specified complexity as proof of intelligence, *when it suits their ideology*. This shows once more how one's biases and assumptions affect one's interpretations of any data. See "God and the Extraterrestrials" for more SETI/UFO fallacies.[3]

LIFE FITS THE DESIGN CRITERION

Life is also characterized by high specified complexity. The leading evolutionary origin-of-life researcher, Leslie Orgel, confirmed this:

> Living things are distinguished by their specified complexity. Crystals such as granite fail to qualify as living because they lack complexity; mixtures of random polymers fail to qualify because they lack specificity.[4]

Unfortunately, a materialist like Orgel here refuses to make the connection between specified complexity and design, even though this is the precise criterion of design.

To elaborate, a *crystal* is a repetitive arrangement of atoms, so is *ordered*. Such ordered structures usually have the lowest energy, so will form spontaneously at low enough temperatures. And the information of the crystals is already present in their building blocks; for example, directional forces between atoms. But proteins and DNA, the most important large molecules of life, are not ordered (in the sense of repetitive), but have high *specified complexity*. Without specification external to the system, i.e., the programmed machinery of

---

3. W. Gitt, "God and the Extraterrestrials," *Creation Ex Nihilo*, 19(4):46–48, September–November 1997.

4. L. Orgel, *The Origins of Life* (New York: John Wiley, 1973), p. 189.

living things or the intelligent direction of an organic chemist, there is no natural tendency to form such complex specified arrangements at all. When their building blocks are combined (and even this requires special conditions[5]), a *random* sequence is the result. The difference between a crystal and DNA is like the difference between a book containing nothing but ABCD repeated and a book of Shakespeare. However, this doesn't stop many evolutionists (ignorant of Orgel's distinction) claiming that crystals prove that specified complexity can arise naturally — they merely prove that *order* can arise naturally, which no creationist contests.[6]

INFORMATION

The design criterion may also be described in terms of *information. Specified complexity* means high *information content*. In formal terms, the information content of any arrangement is the size, in bits, of the shortest algorithm (program) required to generate that arrangement. A random sequence could be formed by a short program:

> (1) Print any letter at random.
> (2) Return to step 1.

A repetitive sequence could be made by the program:

> (1) Print ABCD.
> (2) Return to step 1.

But to print the plays of Shakespeare, a program

5. J. Sarfati. "Origin of Life: The Polymerization Problem," *Creation Ex Nihilo Technical Journal,* 12(3):281–283, 1998.

6. An extensive discussion on information and thermodynamics, order and complexity, is found in C.B. Thaxton, W.L. Bradley, and R.L. Olsen, *The Mystery of Life's Origin* (New York: Philosophical Library, Inc., 1984), chapter 8.

would need to be large enough to print every letter in the right place.[7]

The information content of living things is far greater than that of Shakespeare's writings. The atheist Dawkins says:

> [T]here is enough information capacity in a single human cell to store the *Encyclopedia Britannica*, all 30 volumes of it, three or four times over.[8]

If it's unreasonable to believe that an encyclopedia could have originated without intelligence, then it's just as unreasonable to believe that life could have originated without intelligence.

Even more amazingly, living things have by far the most compact information storage/retrieval system known. This stands to reason if a microscopic cell stores as much information as several sets of *Encyclopedia Britannica*. To illustrate further, the amount of information that could be stored in a pinhead's volume of DNA is staggering. It is the equivalent information content of a pile of paperback books 500 times as tall as the distance from earth to the moon, each with a different, yet specific content.[9]

---

7. Information can be defined mathematically in a way that distinguishes randomness, order, and specified complexity. In terms of signal transmission, a receiver may exist in a large number of possible states (W_0); after a message has been received, the number of possible states drops to W_1. The information content of the message $I_1 = k \ln (W_0/W_1)$, where k = Boltzmann's constant. From M.W. Zemansky, *Heat and Thermodynamics*, 4th ed.(New York: McGraw-Hill, 1975), p. 190. Note that the definition is consistent: with a repetitive sequence, there is a restriction of possibilities, so W_0 is low, so the information is low. Random sequences also contain little information, because there are many possible random sequences (so W_1 is almost as large as W_0).

8. R. Dawkins, *The Blind Watchmaker* (New York: W.W. Norton, 1986), p. 115.

9. W. Gitt, "Dazzling Design in Miniature," *Creation Ex Nihilo,* 20(1):6, December 1997–February 1998.

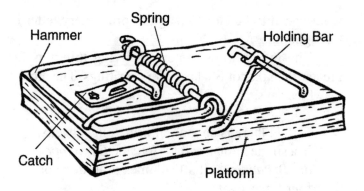

MACHINERY IN LIVING THINGS

On a practical level, information specifies the many parts needed to make machines work. Often, the removal of one part can disrupt the whole machine, so there is a minimum number of parts without which the machine will not work. Biochemist Michael Behe, in his book *Darwin's Black Box*, calls this minimum number *irreducible complexity*.[10] He gives the example of a very simple machine: a mousetrap. This would not work without a platform, holding bar, spring, hammer, and catch, all in the right place. If you remove just one part, it won't work at all — you cannot reduce its complexity without destroying its function entirely.

The thrust of Behe's book is that many structures in living organisms show irreducible complexity, far in excess of a mousetrap or indeed any man-made machine. For example, he shows that even the simplest form of vision in any living creature requires a dazzling array of chemicals in the right places, as well as a system to transmit and process the information. The blood-clotting mechanism also has many different chemicals

---

10. M.J. Behe, *Darwin's Black Box: The Biochemical Challenge to Evolution*, (New York: The Free Press, 1996).

working together, so we won't bleed to death from minor cuts, nor yet suffer from clotting of the entire system.

A SIMPLE CELL?

Many people don't realize that even the simplest cell is fantastically complex —even the simplest self-reproducing organism contains encyclopedic quantities of complex, specific information. *Mycoplasma genitalium* has the smallest known genome of any free-living organism, containing 482 genes comprising 580,000 base pairs[11] (compare 3 billion base pairs in humans, as *Teaching about Evolution* states on page 42). Of course, these genes are functional only in the presence of pre-existing translational and replicating machinery, a cell membrane, etc. But *Mycoplasma* can only survive by parasitizing other more complex organisms, which provide many of the nutrients it cannot manufacture for itself. So evolutionists must postulate a more complex first living organism with even more genes.

More recently, Eugene Koonin and others tried to calculate the bare minimum requirement for a living cell, and came up with a result of 256 genes. But they were doubtful whether such a hypothetical bug could survive, because such an organism could barely repair DNA damage, could no longer fine-tune the ability of its remaining genes, would lack the ability to digest complex compounds, and would need a comprehensive supply of organic nutrients in its environment.[12]

Molecular biologist Michael Denton, writing as a non-creationist skeptic of Darwinian evolution, explains what is involved:

---

11. C.M. Fraser et al., "The Minimal Gene Complement of *Mycoplasma genitalium*," *Science*, 270(5235):397–403, October 20, 1995; Perspective by A. Goffeau, "Life With 482 Genes," same issue, p. 445–446.

12. W. Wells, "Taking Life to Bits," *New Scientist*, 155(2095):30–33, 1997.

Perhaps in no other area of modern biology is the challenge posed by the extreme complexity and ingenuity of biological adaptations more apparent than in the fascinating new molecular world of the cell. . . . To grasp the reality of life as it has been revealed by molecular biology, we must magnify a cell a thousand million times until it is twenty kilometers in diameter and resembles a giant airship large enough to cover a great city like London or New York. What we would then see would be an object of unparalleled complexity and adaptive design. On the surface of the cell we would see millions of openings, like the port holes of a vast space ship, opening and closing to allow a continual stream of materials to flow in and out. If we were to enter one of these openings we would find ourselves in a world of supreme technology and bewildering complexity.

Is it really credible that random processes could have constructed a reality, the smallest element of which — a functional protein or gene — is complex beyond our own creative capacities, a reality which is the very antithesis of chance, which excels in every sense anything produced by the intelligence of man? Alongside the level of ingenuity and complexity exhibited by the molecular machinery of life, even our most advanced artifacts appear clumsy. . . .

It would be an illusion to think that what we are aware of at present is any more than a fraction of the full extent of biological design. In practically every field of fundamental biological research ever-increasing levels of design and complexity are being revealed at an ever-accelerating rate.[13]

For natural selection (differential reproduction) to start, there must be at least one self-reproducing entity. But as shown above, the production of even the simplest cell is beyond the reach of undirected chemical reactions. So it's not surprising that *Teaching about Evolution* omits any discussion of the origin of life, as can easily be seen from the index. However, this is part of the "General Theory of Evolution" (molecules to man),[14] and is often called "chemical evolution." Indeed, the origin of the first self-reproducing system is recognized by many scientists as an unsolved problem for evolution, and thus evidence for a Creator.[15] The chemical hurdles that non-living matter must overcome to form life are insurmountable, as shown by many creationist writers.[16]

CAN MUTATIONS GENERATE INFORMATION?

Even if we grant evolutionists the first cell, the problem of increasing the total information content remains. To go from the first cell to a human means finding a way to generate enormous amounts of information —

13. M. Denton, *Evolution: A Theory in Crisis* (Chevy Chase, MD: Adler and Adler Publishers, Inc., 1986), p. 328, 342.

14. G.A. Kerkut, *Implications of Evolution* (Oxford, UK: Pergamon, 1960). Kerkut, an evolutionist, wrote on p. 157: "There is the theory that all the living forms in the world have arisen from a single source which itself came from an inorganic form. This theory can be called the 'General Theory of Evolution' and the evidence which supports this is not sufficiently strong to allow us to consider it as anything more than a working hypothesis."

15. G. Easterbrook, "Science and God: A Warming Trend?" *Science*, 277(5328):890–893, 1997.

16. S.E. Aw, "The Origin of Life: A Critique of Current Scientific Models," *Creation Ex Nihilo Technical Journal*, 10(3):300–314, 1996; J.D. Sarfati, "Self-Replicating Enzymes?" *Creation Ex Nihilo Technical Journal*, 11(1):4–6, 1997; C.B. Thaxton, W.L. Bradley, and R.L. Olsen, *The Mystery of Life's Origin* (New York: Philosophical Library, Inc., 1984; W.R. Bird, *The Origin of Species: Revisited* (Nashville, TN: Thomas Nelson, Inc., 1991), Vol. 1, Part 3.

billions of base pairs ("letters") worth. This includes the recipes to build eyes, nerves, skin, bones, muscles, blood, etc. In the section on variation and evolution, we showed that evolution relies on copying errors and natural selection to generate the required new information. However, the examples of "contemporary evolution" presented by *Teaching about Evolution* are all *losses* of information.

This is confirmed by the biophysicist Dr. Lee Spetner, who taught information and communication theory at Johns Hopkins University:

> In this chapter I'll bring several examples of evolution, [i.e., instances alleged to be examples of evolution] particularly mutations, and show that information is not increased. . . . But in all the reading I've done in the life-sciences literature, I've never found a mutation that added information.
>
> All point mutations that have been studied on the molecular level turn out to reduce the genetic information and not to increase it.
>
> The NDT [neo-Darwinian theory] is supposed to explain how the information of life has been built up by evolution. The essential biological difference between a human and a bacterium is in the information they contain. All other biological differences follow from that. The human genome has much more information than does the bacterial genome. Information cannot be built up by mutations that lose it. A business can't make money by losing it a little at a time.[17]

17. L. Spetner, *Not by Chance* (Brooklyn, NY: The Judaica Press, Inc.), p. 131–132, 138, 143. See review in *Creation Ex Nihilo*, 20(1):50–51, December 1997–February 1998.

This is not to say that no mutation is "beneficial," that is, it helps the organism to survive. But as pointed out in chapter 2, even increased antibiotic and pesticide resistance is usually the result of *loss* of information, or sometimes a transfer of information — *never* the result of *new* information. Other beneficial mutations include wingless beetles on small desert islands — if beetles lose their wings and so can't fly, the wind is less likely to blow them out to sea.[18] Obviously, this has nothing to do with the origins of flight in the first place, which is what evolution is supposed to be about. Insect flight requires complicated movements to generate the patterns of vortices needed for lift — it took a sophisticated robot to simulate the motion.[19]

WOULD ANY EVIDENCE CONVINCE EVOLUTIONISTS?

The famous British evolutionist (and Communist) J.B.S. Haldane claimed in 1949 that evolution could never produce "various mechanisms, such as the wheel and magnet, which would be useless till fairly perfect."[20] Therefore such machines in organisms would, in his opinion, prove evolution false. That is, evolution meets one criterion *Teaching about Evolution* claims is necessary for science, that there are tests that could conceivably prove it was wrong (the "falsifiability criterion" of the eminent philosopher of science, Karl Popper).

Recent discoveries have shown that there are indeed "wheels" in living organisms. This includes the

---

18. C. Wieland, "Beetle Bloopers," *Creation Ex Nihilo*, 19(3):30, June–August 1997.

19. M. Brookes, "On a wing and a vortex," *New Scientist* 156(2103):24–27, October 11, 1997.

20. Dewar, D., Davies, L.M. and Haldane, J.B.S., (1949). *Is Evolution a Myth? A Debate between D. Dewar and L.M. Davies vs. J.B.S. Haldane*, Watts & Co. Ltd / Paternoster Press, London, p. 90.

rotary motor that drives the flagellum of a bacterium, and the vital enzyme that makes ATP, the "energy currency" of life.[21] These molecular motors have indeed fulfilled one of Haldane's criteria. Also, turtles,[22] monarch butterflies,[23] and bacteria[24] that use magnetic sensors for navigation seem to fulfil Haldane's other criterion.

I wonder whether Haldane would have had a change of heart if he had been alive to see these discoveries. Most evolutionists rule out intelligent design *a priori*, so the evidence, overwhelming as it is, would probably have no effect.

OTHER MARVELS OF DESIGN

- The genetic information in the DNA cannot be translated except with many different enzymes, which are themselves encoded. So the code cannot be translated except via products of translation, a vicious circle that ties evolutionary origin-of-life theories in knots. These include double-sieve enzymes to make sure the right amino acid is linked to the right tRNA. One sieve rejects amino acids too large, while the other rejects those too small.[25]

- The genetic code that's almost universal to life on

---

21. J.D. Sarfati, "Design in Living Organisms: Motors," *Creation Ex Nihilo Technical Journal*, 12(1):3–5, 1998.

22. "Turtles — Reading Magnetic Maps" *Creation Ex Nihilo* 21(2):30, March–May 1999.

23. J.H. Poirier, "The Magnificent Migrating Monarch," *Creation Ex Nihilo*, 20(1):28-31, December 1997–February 1998. But monarchs only use the earth's magnetic field to give them the general direction, while they rely on the sun's position for most of their navigation.

24. M. Helder, "The World's Smallest Compasses," *Creation Ex Nihilo,* 20(2):52–53, March–May 1998.

25. Osamu Nureki et al., "Enzyme Structure with Two Catalytic Sites for Double-sieve Selection of Substrate," *Science,* 280(5363):578–82, April 24, 1998; perspective by A.R. Fersht, "Sieves in Sequence," same issue, p. 541.

J.D. Sarfati, "Decoding and Editing Design: Double Sieve Enzymes, *Creation Ex Nihilo Technical Journal*, 13(1):5–7, 1999.

Earth is about the best possible, for protecting against errors.[26]

- The genetic code also has vital editing machinery that is itself encoded in the DNA. This shows that the system was fully functional from the beginning — another vicious circle for evolutionists.

- Yet another vicious circle, and there are many more, is that the enzymes that make the amino acid histidine themselves contain histidine.

- The complex compound eyes of some types of trilobites (extinct and supposedly "primitive" invertebrates) were amazingly designed. They comprised tubes that each pointed to a different spot on the horizon, and had special lenses that focused light from any distance. Some trilobites had a sophisticated lens design comprising a layer of calcite on top of a layer of chitin — materials with precisely the right refractive indices — and a wavy boundary between them of a precise mathematical shape.[27] The Designer of these eyes is a Master Physicist, who applied what we now know as the physical laws of Fermat's principle of least time, Snell's law of refraction, Abbé's sine law and birefringent optics.

- Lobster eyes are unique in being modeled on a perfect square with precise geometrical relationships of the units. NASA X-ray telescopes copied this design.[28]

---

26. J. Knight, "Top Translator," *New Scientist,* 158(2130):15, April 18, 1998.

27. K. Towe, "Trilobite Eyes: Calcified Lenses," *Science* 179:1007–11, March 9, 1973; R. Levi-Setti, *Trilobites: A Photographic Atlas* (Chicago, IL: University of Chicago Press, 1975). See also C. Stammers, "Trilobite Technology," *Creation Ex Nihilo,* 21(1):37, December 1998–February 1999.

28. M. Chown, "X-ray Lens Brings Finer Chips into Focus," *New Scientist,* 151(2037):18, July 6, 1996.

- The amazing sonar system of dolphins was discussed in chapter 5. Many bats also have an exquisitely designed sonar system. The echolocation of fishing bats is able to detect a minnow's fin, as fine as a human hair, extending only 2 mm above the water surface. This fine detection is possible because bats can distinguish ultra-sound echoes very close together. Man-made sonar can distinguish echoes 12 millionths of a second apart, although with "a lot of work this can be cut to 6 millionths to 8 millionths of a second." But bats "relatively easily" distinguish ultra-sound echoes only 2 to 3 millionths of a second apart according to researcher James Simmons of Brown University. This means they can distinguish objects "just 3/10ths of a millimeter apart — about the width of a pen line on paper."[29]

- The neural system of a leech uses trigonometric calculations to work out which muscles to move and by how much.[30]

- From my own specialist field of vibrational spectroscopy: there is good evidence that our chemical-detecting sense (smell) works on the same quantum mechanical principles.[31]

---

29. Simmons was cited in the appropriately titled article, "Bats Put Technology to Shame," *Cincinnati Enquirer*, October 13, 1998. His research paper is J.A. Simmons et al., "Echo-delay Resolution in Sonar Images of the Big Brown Bat, *Eptesicus fuscus*," *Proceedings of the National Academy of Science USA*, 95(21): 12647–12652, October 13, 1998. See also P. Weston, "Bats: Sophistication in Miniature," *Creation Ex Nihilo*, 21(1):28–31, December 1998–February 1999.

30. R. Howlett, "Simple Minds," *New Scientist,* 158(2139):28–32, June 20, 1998. The editorial on p. 3 of the same issue displayed its materialistic bias by asserting, without the slightest evidence: "The leech's nerve cells arrived at trigonometry by an obviously random and undirected search — evolution, whereas humans seem to have acquired maths by intellectual effort."

31. L. Turin, "A Spectroscopic Mechanism for Primary Olfactory Reception," *Chemical Senses,* 21:773, 1996; cited in S. Hill, "Sniff 'n'shake," *New Scientist,* 157(2115):34–37, January 3, 1998. See also J.D. Sarfati, "Olfactory Design: Smell and Spectroscopy," *Creation Ex Nihilo Technical Journal*, 12(2):137–8, 1998.

WHY SHOULD DESIGN BE "UNSCIENTIFIC"?

The real reason for rejecting the creation explanation is the commitment to naturalism. As shown in chapter 1, evolutionists have turned science into a materialistic "game," and creation/design is excluded by their self-serving rules.[32] Therefore, although *Teaching about Evolution* dismisses creation science as "unscientific," this appears to be derived more from the rules of the game than from any evidence.

Even some anti-creationist philosophers of science have strongly criticized the evolutionary scientific and legal establishment over these word games. They rightly point out that we should be more interested in whether creation is *true* or *false* than whether it meets some self-serving criteria for "science."[33]

Many of these word games are self-contradictory, so one must wonder whether their main purpose is to exclude creation at any cost, rather than for logical reasons. For example, *Teaching about Evolution* claims on page 55:

> The ideas of "creation science" derive from the conviction that God created the universe — including humans and other living things — all at once in the relatively recent past. However, scientists from many fields have examined these ideas and have found them to be scientifically insupportable. For

---

32. C. Wieland, "Science: The Rules of the Game," *Creation Ex Nihilo*, 11(1):47–50, December 1988–February 1989.

33. M. Ruse, editor, *But Is it Science?* "Science at the Bar — Causes for Concern," by L. Laudan and "The Philosopher of Science as Expert Witness," by P.L. Quinn (Buffalo, NY: Prometheus Books, 1988), p. 351–355, 367–385. Ruse was the philosopher of science who most influenced American judges that creation is "unscientific," and Laudan and Quinn, themselves evolutionists, refute his fallacious arguments.

example, evidence for a very young earth is incompatible with many different methods of establishing the age of rocks. Furthermore, because the basic proposals of creation science are not subject to test and verification, these ideas do not meet the criteria for science.

The *Teaching about Evolution* definition of creation science is almost right, although creationists following biblical assumptions would claim that different things were created on different days. However, *Teaching about Evolution* claims that the ideas of creation science have been examined and found unsupportable, then they claim that the "basic proposals of creation science are not subject to test and verification." So how could its proposals have been examined (tested!) if they are not subject to test?

Of course, it is not true that science has proved the earth to be billions of years old — see chapter 8.

The historian and philosopher of science Stephen Meyer concluded:

We have not yet encountered any good in principle reason to exclude design from science. Design seems just as scientific (or unscientific) as its evolutionary competitors. . . .

An openness to empirical arguments for design is therefore a necessary condition of a fully rational historical biology. A rational historical biology must not only address the question, "Which materialistic or naturalistic evolutionary scenario provides the most adequate explanation of biological complexity?" but also the question "Does a strictly materialistic evolutionary scenario or one involving intelligent agency or some other theory best explain the origin of biological complexity, given all relevant evidence?" To insist otherwise is to insist that materialism holds a metaphysically privileged position. Since there seems no reason to concede that assumption, I see no reason to concede that origins theories must be strictly naturalistic.[34]

---

34. J.P. Moreland, editor, *The Creation Hypothesis,* "The Methodological Equivalence of Design and Descent: Can There Be a 'Scientific Theory of Creation?' " by S.C. Meyer (Downers Grove, IL: InterVarsity Press, 1994), p. 98, 102.

CHAPTER 10

CONCLUSION

This book has addressed the main arguments for evolution presented by *Teaching about Evolution and the Nature of Science* and found them wanting. By contrast, the evidence for creation is cogent. In particular, *Refuting Evolution* has covered the following areas in its nine chapters:

1. Facts do not speak for themselves, but must be *interpreted* according to a framework. The leading evolutionists are biased towards naturalism, to the extent that many are outspoken atheists. This is especially true of the National Academy of Science, the producers of *Teaching about Evolution.* Conversely, creationists admit that they are biased in favor of creation as revealed in the Bible. Although they have the *same* facts as evolutionists, interpreting them according to a biblical framework results in a more scientifically cogent theory.

2. Adherents to both the biblical creation/corruption/ flood framework and the particles-to-people evolution framework teach that organisms change through time, and that mutations and natural selection play a

large part in this. But evolutionists assume that the changes eventually increase the information content, so that a single living cell (which they claim arose from non-living chemicals) was the ancestor of all other life. Creationists believe that separate kinds were created, and that changes generally either remove information or leave the total information content unchanged. The examples of "evolution in action" presented by *Teaching about Evolution* do *not* demonstrate the information increase required by evolution. Rather, they are examples of variation within a kind, and are consistent with the creation framework.

3. Evolutionists since Darwin have predicted that the fossil record would show many intermediate forms linking one kind of organism to a different kind. Instead, the fossil record shows that animals appear abruptly and fully formed, with only a handful of debatable examples of alleged transitional forms. It is also doubtful whether one can even imagine functional intermediates in many cases.

4. Birds are unique creatures, with wings and feathers designed for flight, and special lungs completely different from those of any reptile. Some evolutionists propose that birds evolved from gliding tree reptiles, while others propose that birds evolved from running dinosaurs. Each group refutes the other so convincingly that a reasonable conclusion is that birds did not evolve from non-birds at all.

5. Whales are mammals designed for life in water, with many unique features. *Teaching about Evolution* asserts that whales evolved from land animals, and presents an alleged series of whale intermediates. But on close analysis, none stands up. For example, we

find that the fossil evidence for one alleged key intermediate, *Ambulocetus*, is fragmentary. Another alleged intermediate, *Basilosaurus*, is actually 10 times the size of *Ambulocetus* although the book draws them the same size. And an evolutionary vertebrate paleontologist points out its peculiar body and tooth shape mean that *Basilosaurus* "could not possibly have been the ancestor of modern whales."

6. Humans are very different from apes, especially in intelligence and language. *Teaching about Evolution* presents a series of alleged "ape-man" skulls. But the evidence shows that humans and australopithecines are distinct kinds. This includes analysis of the semicircular canals in the ear and the canal that carried the nerve to the tongue. DNA similarities between humans and chimps are exaggerated; the dissimilarities correspond to encyclopedic differences in information. A common creator is a better explanation for both similarities and differences. Proper drawings of embryos show that different kinds have very different embryos, not similar ones, despite the claim of *Teaching about Evolution*.

7. *Teaching about Evolution* presents the usual "big bang" theory. However, there is no satisfactory evolutionary explanation to explain how the universe could come into existence without a cause, or for the formation of stars and solar systems after such an alleged "big bang." *Teaching about Evolution* also discusses the Galileo controversy, but misses the point. The Church had adopted the Ptolemaic framework and interpreted the Bible accordingly. Secular defenders of the framework persuaded the Church leaders that Galileo was really contradicting the Bible. Moreover, the verses (mis)used to teach Ptolemaic astronomy were often from the Psalms, Hebrew

poetry (unlike Genesis) that was clearly not intended to teach a particular cosmological model. Also, other biblical passages (mis)used were using the earth as a *reference frame*, a scientifically accurate procedure.

8. *Teaching about Evolution* teaches that the earth is billions of years old, and uses the fossils and radiometric dating as "proof." However, there is evidence that many rocks and fossils were formed by catastrophic processes, which is consistent with the biblical framework that includes a global flood. Radiometric dating theory relies on several untestable assumptions about the past, and the methods have often proven false and even self-contradictory in practice. Ninety percent of the methods that have been used to estimate the age of the earth indicate an age far younger than that asserted by *Teaching about Evolution*.

9. Living organisms have encyclopedic quantities of complex, specific information coded in the DNA. Interestingly, this is precisely the criterion that would prove that a signal from outer space has an intelligent source. DNA itself is the most efficient storage/retrieval system in the universe. The information it stores is the blueprint for all the enzymes required for life, and the recipe for building the complex organs needed. Some of these include sonars of dolphins and bats, and the miniature motors driving flagella or making the ATP molecule. These are far more complex than anything humans have built. Other structures have inspired human inventions; for example, the lobster eye inspired an x-ray telescope design. Finally, it is shown that the design explanation is legitimate, and that the only reason to reject it is an *a priori* faith in materialism.

Thus, there is good reason to take the biblical creationist framework seriously, and every reason that students should hear the evidence against evolution.

For a free catalog of material supporting biblical creation, or for more information about what the Bible teaches, contact one of the Answers in Genesis ministries below. Answers in Genesis ministries are evangelical, Christ-centered, non-denominational, and non-profit.

Answers in Genesis *(USA)*
P.O. Box 6330
Florence
Kentucky 41022
USA

Answers in Genesis *(Australia)*
P.O. Box 6302
Acacia Ridge DC
QLD 4110
Australia

Answers in Genesis *(Canada)*
5-420 Erb St. West Suite 213
Waterloo, Ontario
Canada N2L 6K6

Answers in Genesis *(NZ)*
P.O. Box 39005
Howick
Auckland
New Zealand

Answers in Genesis *(UK)*
P.O. Box 5262
Leicester
LE2 3XU
United Kingdom

Answers in Genesis *(Japan)*
Attn: Nao Hanada
3317-23 Nagaoka, Ibaraki-machi
Higashi-ibaraki-gun, Ibaraki-ken 311-3116
Japan

INDEX

ABOUT THE AUTHOR

Jonathan D. Sarfati, Ph.D, F.M., was born in Ararat, Australia, in 1964. He moved to New Zealand as a child, where he later studied mathematics, geology, physics, and chemistry at Victoria University in Wellington. He obtained honors level in physical and inorganic chemistry, as well as in condensed matter physics and nuclear physics.

He received his Ph.D. in physical chemistry from the same institution in 1995 on the topic of spectroscopy, especially vibrational. He has co-authored various technical papers on such things as high temperature superconductors and sulfur and selenium-containing ring and cage molecules.

As well as being very interested in formal logic and philosophy, Dr. Sarfati is a keen chess player. He represented New Zealand in three Chess Olympiads and is a former New Zealand national chess champion. In 1988, F.I.D.E., the International Chess Federation, awarded him the title of F.I.D.E. Master (F.M.).

A Christian since 1984, he was for some years on the editorial committee of *Apologia*, the journal of the Wellington Christian Apologetics Society, of which he was a co-founder.

Dr. Sarfati currently works full-time for Answers in Genesis in Brisbane, Australia, a non-profit ministry, as a research scientist and editorial consultant for *Creation Ex Nihilo* family magazine and the associated *Technical Journal*, and has written many articles for both. He also contributes to the Answers in Genesis Internet website, particularly the 'Hot Topics' section.